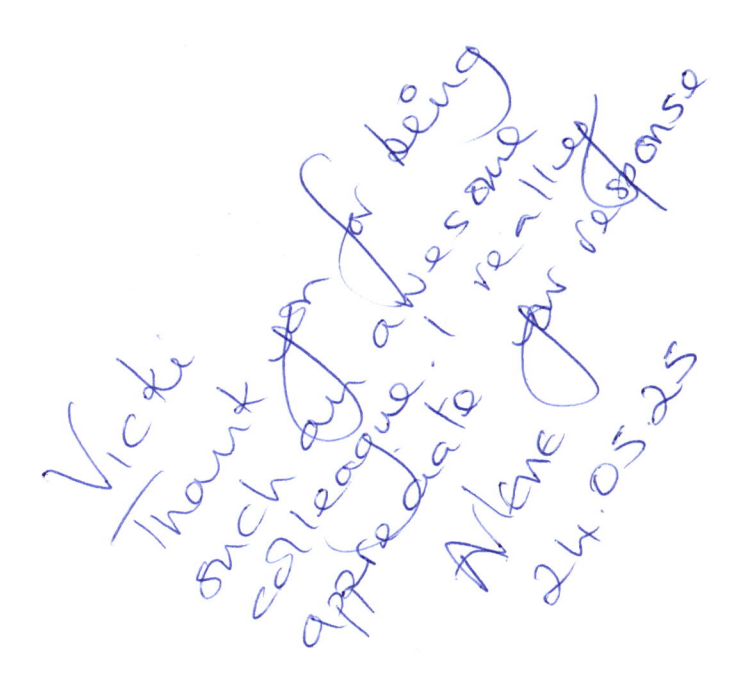

Effective Personal and Professional Judgement in Social Work

How personal biography can affect professional effectiveness

*Vicki,
Thank you for being such an awesome colleague. I really appreciate your response
Arlene
24.05.25*

Effective Personal and Professional Judgement in Social Work

How personal biography can affect professional effectiveness

Arlene P Weekes | **Denise Harvey**

Routledge
Taylor & Francis Group
LONDON AND NEW YORK

Designed cover images: Krakenimages/AdobeStock
Cover design by Out of House Limited

First published 2025
by Routledge
4 Park Square, Milton Park, Abingdon, Oxon OX14 4RN

and by Routledge
605 Third Avenue, New York, NY 10158

Routledge is an imprint of the Taylor & Francis Group, an informa business

© 2025 Arlene P Weekes and Denise Harvey

The right of Arlene P Weekes and Denise Harvey to be identified as authors of this work has been asserted in accordance with sections 77 and 78 of the Copyright, Designs and Patents Act 1988.

All rights reserved. No part of this book may be reprinted or reproduced or utilised in any form or by any electronic, mechanical, or other means, now known or hereafter invented, including photocopying and recording, or in any information storage or retrieval system, without permission in writing from the publishers.

Trademark notice: Product or corporate names may be trademarks or registered trademarks, and are used only for identification and explanation without intent to infringe.

British Library Cataloguing in Publication Data
A CIP record for this book is available from the British Library

ISBN: 9781915713728 (pbk)
ISBN: 9781041055259 (ebk)

DOI: 10.4324/9781041055259

Text design by Greensplash
Typeset in 10/14 Cambria
by Newgen Publishing UK

Acknowledgements

We acknowledge with gratitude our fore parents, whose legacy of faith, wisdom and storytelling, grounded in Africa-centredness, has been passed down through the generations. Their teachings have provided us with a foundation, which we have intertwined with our Western education to create this book.

It aims to support students and social workers in their careers, encouraging them to strive for integrity in their social work practice. It stands as a testament to the principles and values instilled in us by those who came before and is dedicated to those who will come after us. We are humbled to share it with the world.

Endorsement

Decision-making is central to effective social work and affects the lives of service-users and their families. As social workers, each of us brings our own history to the task, which influences our assumptions and interpretations in ways that we rarely fully understand. We are often unaware of our assumptions until we encounter a situation that challenges them, often in uncomfortable ways and with potentially unfortunate consequences. This book provides a rare opportunity for us to discover how our personal history affects our decision-making in a non-threatening way where we can feel safe to reflect and learn without becoming defensive. The concept of unconscious bias is often discussed but poorly understood. The authors draw upon a deep theoretical base to understand how the unconscious influences our everyday thinking. Drawing upon findings from research and from public inquiries and serious case reviews, they go on to highlight how decision-making can go wrong and how this can be avoided. The exercises are thought-provoking and support us to become more empathetic and more open to sharing ourselves and our experiences in an appropriate way. This book is highly relevant to experienced practitioners and managers as to students on social work and other relevant courses. It is likely to become a 'must read' for effective self-development.

Andrew Whittaker PhD
Professor of Social Work Research
London South Bank University

Contents

	About the authors	*xi*
	Introduction: why is this book important?	1
Chapter 1	Effective Personal and Professional Judgement (EPPJ): the foundation research	5
Chapter 2	Basic ideas: theoretical conceptualisations	13
Chapter 3	Exploring faith and identity: how different religions shape values and behaviour	47
Chapter 4	The 'wounded healer' and the consciousness/constructiveness axle	65
Chapter 5	Factors affecting decision-making processes	83
Chapter 6	Group decision-making processes	93
Chapter 7	Applying EPPJ	107
Chapter 8	Benefits of EPPJ	123
Chapter 9	Identifying your category: the EPPJ web tool	141
Chapter 10	A unified approach: the future of EPPJ within and across disciplines	149
	Glossary	*165*
	References	*171*
	Index	*181*

About the **authors**

Arlene P Weekes has 34 years' experience in social work, primarily in senior management roles. She is a published author, an independent fostering panel chair, a management and training consultant, and director of EPPJ Ltd. Over the last four years, she has been a senior university lecturer (SFHEA), leading modules on readiness for direct practice, understanding equality and diversity for social work practice and ethics, human rights for social work practice and effective multi-agency working, utilising student-centred, constructivist and action learning pedagogies. Arlene's research interests include race (specifically Black women), religion, the impact of values on decision-making and student engagement. Her PhD research focused on how individuals' biographies, attitudes and values influence the decision-making processes, emphasising the importance of self-awareness and managing both conscious and unconscious influences. Arlene developed the Effective Personal and Professional Judgement (EPPJ) framework, which is aimed at improving decision-making by understanding internal and external influences.

Denise Harvey is a qualified social worker with over 21 years' experience working in various areas of children and families' services. She is a fellow of the higher education academy (FHEA) and professional lead for social work at London South Bank University. Having significant current practice experience in both the Youth Court and the Family Court, she uses her practice skills as lead on the undergraduate Law for Social Work module. Denise is an experienced and published researcher whose areas of expertise include youth justice law, risk and decision-making. She is currently completing her PhD.

Introduction: why is this book important?

Every aspect of our lives involves an element of the thinking process. Often this thinking is unconscious, such as when we carry out routine, familiar tasks. On other occasions, our thinking is conscious, such as when we need to perform tasks that require us to make informed decisions. Such tasks can range from deciding our personal career goals and which school our children should attend to whether we exercise today or go out for a meal. However, although humans are continuously involved in the act of thinking, either consciously or unconsciously, it is wrong to assume that any decision-making processes are simple, rational and objective. There are many studies from the fields of psychotherapy and psychology showing that the decision-making process is extremely complex and our thinking apparatus is heavily influenced by our personal experiences, dating back to birth.

The result of the influence of our personal experiences (our 'biography') on our thinking is far reaching. It affects everything we do, from the places where we choose to live to the friends we make and the people we date. It is clear from many studies, including Weekes (2021), that our biography also has a real and significant effect on our decision-making. Research on juries, for example, has shown that jurors interpret and evaluate information in a biased way, as a result of prior beliefs and personal experience, and often fail to take the instructions of the judge into consideration (Carlson and Russo, 2001). Jurors are also often swayed by being in a group as, according to Pigott and Foley (1995), they are inclined to change their original views in favour of a majority decision in line with the views of other jurors. This is known as 'groupthink'. Another study (Bornstein and Miller, 2009) identified that judges are also influenced by their personal biography, with a judge's religion and other background factors affecting decision-making.

Background to the book

This book outlines a recently developed method for improving decision-making processes within social work by minimising the effects of personal biography. It is based on recent research and is designed to support the Effective Personal Professional Judgement (EPPJ) online tool. The need for real improvement in decision-making in the public care system was highlighted in *Independent Review of Children's Social Care: The Case for Change* (2022): 'By having clearer and more accountable multi-agency arrangements we enable better ... decision making about children' (p 96).

This book provides you with a comprehensive and in-depth exploration of the causes and effects of personal biography, which enables you to challenge your own biases. It allows you to engage with your personal biography and the effect of this on bias. It accepts that in the real world of professional decision-making, this is impossible. Instead, it describes a method called Effective Personal Professional Judgement (EPPJ), which recognises the existence of bias and seeks to minimise its effect on the decision-making process by directing you to increase self-awareness. The aim is to help those who make decisions about others and processes to do this fairly and in a more objective and balanced way than they would otherwise. Improvement, rather than perfection, is the goal.

Although EPPJ was developed for use in the social work context, it is relevant to many professional environments, especially those that include an active involvement in the decision-making process. It should also be noted that although the ideas in this book are presented against a UK background, they are applicable in all countries.

Structure of the book

To give you an idea of the topics that are covered in this book, each chapter is briefly introduced here.

- » Chapter 1 outlines the foundational research that led to the EPPJ framework.
- » Chapter 2 considers the basic ideas and theoretical concepts.
- » Chapter 3 examines how faith and religion shape identity.
- » Chapter 4 explores the idea of the 'wounded healer' and looks at the EPPJ's consciousness/constructiveness axis.
- » Chapter 5 explores factors that affect the decision-making process.
- » Chapter 6 looks at group decision-making processes.
- » Chapter 7 presents the application of EPPJ.
- » Chapter 8 outlines the benefits of EPPJ.
- » Chapter 9 allows you to interact with EPPJ and use the tool to find your personal EPPJ category.
- » Chapter 10 explores the future of EPPJ.

We have included a full glossary, index and reference list so you can explore further reading. Throughout each chapter, there are also opportunities to capture personal reflection and individual thoughts.

Structure of each chapter

We start each chapter by introducing you to a key concept and we use case studies to illustrate relevant concepts as we go through. There are opportunities for you to reflect on what you have learned and for you to make notes of personal thoughts. Following this, we leave you with a chapter summary and conclude with key takeaways.

And finally ...

We hope that by engaging with this book you are able to reflect openly and honestly on the personal biases that you bring to every decision you make, not only professionally but personally. As outlined above, perfection is not the end goal; rather, you should aim for improvement and an ability to look at yourself and understand what you can bring to every situation you encounter.

Chapter 1 | Effective Personal Professional Judgement (EPPJ): the foundation research

If they wanna make the world a better place
Take a look at yourself and then make a change.

Glen Ballard and Siedah Garrett (1987)

Introduction

This chapter is intentionally shorter than the others in the book, as the entire book is dedicated to expounding the research that led to the Effective Personal Professional Judgement (EPPJ) framework. It would be remiss not to provide an overall summary of the research; nonetheless, the reader is directed to the References section at the end of the book should they wish to read the two specific journal articles written by the author (Weekes, 2021, 2022).

EPPJ emerged from research undertaken by Dr Arlene P Weekes as a result of her thesis submitted in partial fulfilment of the requirements of her Professional Doctorate in Social Work (Weekes, 2020), which set out to explore the judgements of panel members and panels when recommending who is suitable to become a parent (either temporarily as a foster carer or permanently as an adopter). A summary of the research's aims and findings is provided here, as they are fundamental to the concept of EPPJ (see also Weekes, 2021).

The principal question the research set out to explore was:

» In what ways do adoption and fostering panel members' biographies, attitudes and values influence their roles and recommendation-making?

The sub-questions included:

» What is the underlying thinking of panel members when arriving at their recommendations on the suitability/approval of foster carers/adopters and matches?

» In what ways do adoption and fostering panel members' biographies, attitudes and values influence their role occupancy and recommendation-making?

» To what extent does a panel member's conceptualisation of their professionalism impact their role on the panel?

» What are the systems, methods and techniques that impact recommendations?

» What are the group processes at play when panels make their recommendations?

Developing the EPPJ framework

The objective of the research was to investigate the judgements and recommendations of panel members as they consider and make judgements regarding those who desire to provide care for children known to children's services. In particular, it set out to explore how adoption and fostering panel members' biographies, attitudes and values influence their role and the process of making recommendations. In order to do this, the study looked into the panel members' underlying assumptions when making decisions and the extent to which they considered that their professionalism influenced their roles. Additionally, it examined the procedures, techniques and group dynamics that affect panel recommendations.

Methodology

The objective was to investigate and evaluate the ways in which people's conscious and unconscious influences impact their ability to make recommendations. Using narrative interviews based on Wengraf's (2004) Biographic Narrative Interpretive Method (BNIM), the transcripts were examined analysing how each individual constructed meaning from their personal experiences, life histories and lived situations. The study evaluated each narrative study separately and collectively (cross-case theorisation) by examining the parallels and divergences before discovering recurring themes. The EPPJ framework was built on earlier research.

Individual and collective decision-making

Wilfred Bion's 1962 work on the concept of the 'link' in thinking refers to the relationship between thoughts and the mental processes that shape them, where emotional experiences are transformed into thoughts through a dynamic connection between the thinker and their internal or external objects, either in a positive (knowledge-seeking) or negative (defensive or destructive) direction.

Bion's (1962) work identified two basic categories of groups: the 'workgroup', distinguished by a high degree of cooperation; and the 'basic assumption group', referring to unconscious, collective behaviours in a group that override rational thought and task-focused functioning. These basic assumptions, such as dependency, fight/flight and pairing, reflect primitive emotional needs and defences, causing the group to act as if it exists to fulfil these unconscious desires rather than its stated purpose.

Janis's (1982) 'groupthink' is another group phenomenon analysis that sees a well-designed group as having the ability to make more effective choices; this potential advantage is frequently lost when the members work closely together because of the psychological pressure that arises from achieving group consensus.

Baron (1994) demonstrates that biased and irrational thinking can also be seen in closed groups, pointing to another group-level behavioural phenomenon that frequently results in poor decision-making.

Theory of decisions

The process of decision-making is at the heart of the study on decision theory (you can revisit these theories in full in Chapter 2). Many pertinent contributions have been made to decision theory, which focuses on the process of decision-making. Lord et al (1979) argue that people make judgements based on stereotypes and personal ideas, and that once these are formed, they do not change. Bodenhausen and Wyer (1985) found that people use stereotype-based impressions when processing information about individuals.

A comparison of jury and judge decision-making

As minimal research had been undertaken on panels, a review of the studies on judge and jury decision-making was undertaken as this process is comparable to panel decision-making in certain ways. For instance, Pennington and Hastie (1992) and Carlson and Russo (2001) agree that jurors rely on preconceived concepts and subjective narratives rather than objective facts in their decision-making processes. The jurors' dependence on personal experiences and biases may lead to skewed interpretations of evidence. Pennington and Hastie (1992) investigate groupthink and jury information assessment, whereas Carlson and Russo (2001) highlight the influence of biases on pre-decisional distortion in evidence processing. Pigott and Foley (1995) found that juries demonstrate diminished personal prejudice during deliberations, but they often modify their initial judgements to conform to the majority verdict. Bornstein and Greene (2011) found that juries use their expertise and experience in assessing evidence, allowing their emotions to influence their choices. Bornstein and Miller (2009) illustrate that judges can allow religious beliefs and other contextual elements to affect their decision-making, thereby contesting the dominant belief that judicial decisions are exclusively grounded in legal principles and evidence.

Findings

Individual thinking and awareness of values and beliefs

Since intuitive (emotional) thinking cannot be completely avoided, the focus should be on honing analytical (cognitive) skills to make sure intuition's acknowledged biases are handled sensibly. In order to address this need, this study looks at the panel members' underlying assumptions and prejudices while formulating recommendations, paying particular attention to how they are affected. This begs the question of whether panel recommendation-making processes can make good use of personal biographies.

The professional context: how people influence and are influenced by teams and meetings

The narratives that emerged from the interviews emphasised the widely established reality that individuals possess intricate backgrounds, perspectives and histories, all of which impact their conduct and the effectiveness of their roles.

The study found that well-managed meetings and organisational environments are less likely to exhibit 'groupthink', which is the propensity to restrict individual freedom of expression for the sake of maintaining group cohesion (Janis, 1982); they are therefore more likely to be effective.

Influencing factors

The study revealed that several meeting/organisational management and facilitation factors have a significant impact. Arguably the most significant of these is leadership. The study found four main themes:

» task focus (capacity to stay on task as opposed to straying from the panel's mandate);

» organisation (before, during and following the panel);

» professionalism;

» examination (high-quality assurance/examination in contrast to a conveyor belt/rubber stamping of suggestions).

One of the main themes of this study is therefore that people are inherently judgemental, with implicit biases affecting them individually as well as when they are in groups. In relation to this, group unity can take precedence over individual freedom. It goes without saying that this 'groupthink', whether it occurs in a group or an individual, is undesirable because it frequently results in poor judgement.

Conclusion

This study set out to investigate how members of adoption and fostering panels' personal histories, attitudes and values affect their roles and recommendation-making. It discovered that panel members' individual biographies had a surprisingly large impact on how well they performed in their roles. Several initiatives have been proposed to address this issue on an individual and collective level.

The study also highlighted that there is evidence in the literature that group decision-making can be more advantageous than individual decision-making in many situations, with a substantial amount of research suggesting that these benefits might be negated by a combination of collective thinking and biases.

According to the research, people's decision-making processes are significantly influenced by their own biographies, impacting both group dynamics and individual judgement.

The study recommended several actions at the individual, group and corporate levels to lessen bias and enhance the integrity of decision-making in order to address both explicit and implicit biases. It becomes clear that in order to ensure efficient operation and discernment in making morally right decisions, strong leadership, task concentration, appropriate structure, professionalism and careful examination are all necessary.

One of the central aims of the study was to investigate the extent to which personal biographies impact individuals' recommendation-making in the panel setting. Effective recommendation-making requires that individuals accept the influence of the unconscious, as well as understanding and managing conscious attitudes. As Carl Jung (1993) observed:

> *Indeed it is sufficiently obvious, and has been confirmed over and over again by experience, that what the doctor fails to see in himself he either will not see at all, or will see grossly exaggerated, in his patient; further, he encourages those things to which he himself unconsciously inclines and condemns everything that he abhors in himself.*

It should be noted that while Jung refers to doctors, nowadays this includes professionals in several helping professionals, including social workers, counsellors, therapists and educators. These occupations frequently necessitate individual interactions with those in need of support, guidance, or care.

Reflective exercise

This exercise promotes personal reflection and application to internalise the EPPJ framework by focusing and reflecting upon your own personal experiences and professional practice. Aimed at promoting self-awareness and practical implementation, it will enable you to personalise your understanding of the framework to improve future decision-making.

Steps

1. Reflect on a past decision:
   » Think of a recent decision made in your personal or professional life – where you had to weigh different factors before concluding.
2. Analyse the decision:
   » What personal values, beliefs and biases influenced the decision?
   » What professional standards, guidelines or responsibilities were considered?
   » How did personal and professional aspects come together in the final decision?
   » Were there any tensions or conflicts?
3. Evaluate using the EPPJ framework:
   » How could you have used the EPPJ framework to enhance your decision-making process?
   » Did you believe you balanced personal and professional judgement effectively? If not, how could the framework have helped?

Reflective questions

» What aspects of personal and professional judgement do you need to focus on developing?
» How can you ensure that you remain objective and reflective in your decision-making?
» What steps will you take to apply the EPPJ framework in your next professional or personal decision?

Chapter summary

The key conclusion of the study was that any belief that individuals can be truly objective is a fallacy, and that effective recommendation-making requires individuals to accept the influence of the unconscious, as well as understanding and managing conscious attitudes. Felix Biestek (1953), a major contributor to the development of modern social work, states:

> The 'non-judgmental attitude' is one of those troublesome terms. Social workers are probably unanimous in considering it a basic concept, but whenever its meaning is discussed in any sizeable group, there are many protestations to the effect that 'that isn't what I mean by the non-judgmental attitude'.

If panel members can be more conscious of their role, they will be more constructive in performing the tasks involved. However, the study found that most panel members are either unaware, or not in control, of their unconscious personality characteristics. The observations made in the study identified several unconscious aspects of personality projected onto workers or applicants. When panel members show an excessively emotional response to any aspect of their work, it indicates the expression of unconscious content through questions, statements or recommendations. A key finding of the study was that very few panel members demonstrated awareness and management of their conscious and unconscious self. The study also found significant evidence that a person's awareness and ability to reflect on their personal history and relationships affects the functioning of panels and decision-making.

Key takeaways from the chapter

- EPPJ is about improving decision-making in social work.
- Our attitudes and values (biography) are key factors in decision-making.
- Our awareness and ability to reflect on our biographies impact our decision-making.
- The more conscious we are of our biographies, the more constructive we are in carrying out tasks.
- EPPJ helps us to develop this consciousness.

Chapter 2 | Basic ideas: theoretical conceptualisations

Our thoughts, feelings and attitudes about particular groups in society [are influenced] by our experiences at a personal level.

Neil Thompson (2017)

Introduction

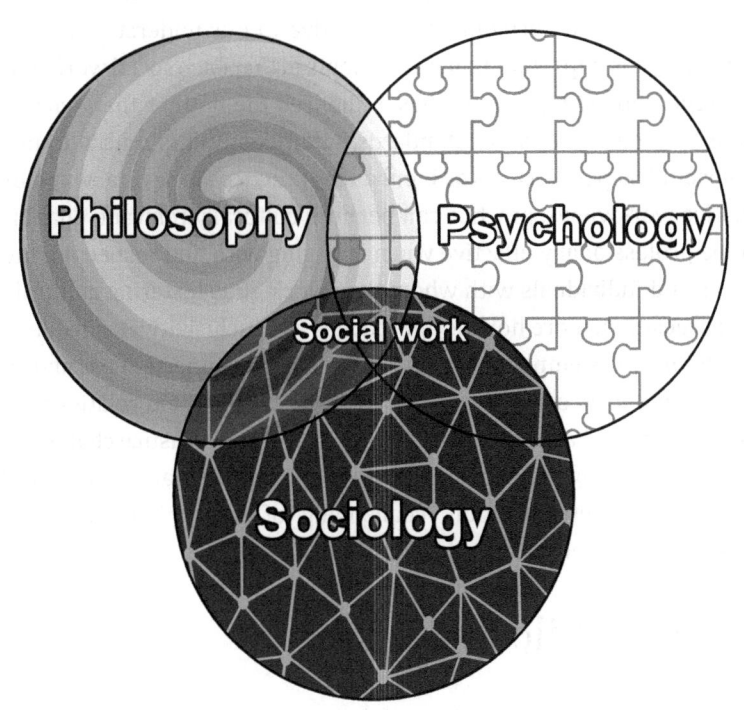

Figure 2.1 Integrated humanities: exploring culture, society and identity

The main purpose of this chapter is to explore and answer the question:

Can social work practitioners and students truly be anti-discriminatory, anti-racist and empowering in their practice, without having an in-depth knowledge of philosophy, psychology and sociology?

Before this question can be answered, it is important to grapple with a few concepts from the fields of psychology, philosophy and sociology. While these disciplines are interlinked and interrelated, they have unique perspectives (see Figure 2.1). Philosophy is more abstract, concerned with the critical examination of the fundamental nature of existence, knowledge, reality, reasoning and values; psychology focuses on understanding individual mentality and behaviours; and sociology investigates society, culture, communities (groupings) and causality.

Philosophy

The study of philosophy is the pursuit of fundamental truths based on the exploration of ideas and issues, encapsulating values, ethics, interconnecting identities and legislative frameworks as we seek to understand ourselves, others and the world we inhabit. To provide a decolonised perspective to our understanding of effective decision-making, it is important that it is recognised that each social worker's perspective is different, depending on what has influenced them other than what they have been taught by their profession's standards. Additionally, it is crucial to incorporate varied philosophical perspectives as it enhances practices in several ways. By providing alternative worldviews, practice can be more culturally relevant, enabling practitioners to be professionally effective when engaging with and respecting the distinct communities and individuals with whom they work, thus fostering cultural humility, a deeper appreciation, more holistic approaches and inclusivity. For instance, African and Asian philosophies emphasise communalism, interconnectedness and social harmony, which can inform social work's focus on community and relationships. Or the critical perspectives of Latin American liberation and social justice challenge Western ideologies, which strongly emphasise autonomy, individual and human rights, personal freedom, self-determination, challenging of discrimination and advocacy through the enactment of social policies and legislation.

Worldwide philosophies

What follows is a brief overview of the philosophical perspectives and philosophers related to values, beliefs, ethics, morality and religion from the different continents (excluding Antarctica) and how they can be applied to social work practice, citing the legislation in some countries to illustrate how ethics and legislation go hand in hand to bring about fairness in social work.

Asia

The continent of Asia has 48 countries divided into five major regions: East, South, Central, Southeast and Western Asia. This chapter focuses on India in the South and China in the East.

Spotlight on key philosophers and concepts

Table 2.1 identifies philosophies from Asia include Confucianism, which stresses virtues such as compassion, familial piety and social relationships, morality and non-violence; Buddhism, with its focus on compassion, mindfulness, the alleviation of suffering through ethical living and detachment from desires and the right path in life; and Daoism, which stresses the importance of harmony with nature, simplicity and the balance between opposing forces (yin and yang). Such philosophies advocate respect for elders, communal well-being and a holistic approach to life. In contrast, Hinduism emphasises the notion of karma and the law of cause and effect – moral responsibility and the associated social consequences. These approaches all focus on the need to balance and embrace diversity; they can culturally inform approaches of humility and emphasise interconnectedness within communities, promoting holistic well-being.

Table 2.1 Key Asian philosophers relevant to social work

	Country	Philosopher	Core perspective relevant to social work
1	China	Confucius (Kong Fuzi) (551–c. 479 BCE)	Focused on ethics, familial loyalty, respect for elders, education and governance based on moral virtues. Confucius's philosophical teachings emphasise the importance of a well-ordered society, righteous conduct, propriety, humanity, social harmony and proper relationships within society.
2	India	Siddhartha Gautama (Buddha) (563–c. 483 BCE)	Renouncing position and wealth to seek enlightenment. Emphasis on mindfulness, resilience, compassion and the alleviation of suffering. By being empathetic, mindful, self-aware and compassionate, one can develop a deeper understanding of self and others through connectedness. Striving for social justice, advocacy to address systematic issues.
3	China	Laozi (Lao Tzu) (sixth century CE)	Developed ideas of Taoism, highlighting the importance of humility, naturalness and simplicity. His viewpoint included balance, moderation and the importance of the inner self.

Africa

The continent of Africa has 54 countries divided among the five regions: Northern Africa, Southern Africa, Central/Middle Africa, East Africa and Western Africa. This chapter focuses on Cameroon, Egypt, Ethiopia, Ghana, Nigeria, Senegal and South Africa.

Spotlight on key philosophers and concepts

African philosophy and philosophers are now being given platform, as can be seen below (see Table 2.2). African philosophies emphasise communalism, the value of community, the importance of communal relationships and interventions, compassion and collective and communal well-being. For example, ubuntu has deep roots in the traditions of Bantu-speaking peoples, dating back to the fifteenth century and beyond, even though the exact origins are unknown.

Table 2.2 Key African philosophers relevant to social work

	Country	Philosopher	Core perspective relevant to social work
1	Egypt (North)	Hypatia (355–415 CE)	Promoted reasoned argument and scientific investigation, introducing neoplatonism, which placed a strong emphasis on using reason and pursuing knowledge.
2	Senegalese (West)	Kocc (Kotch) Barma Fall (1586–1655 CE)	Renowned for his wisdom and pursuit of knowledge, dialogue, critical thinking and insightful proverbs, such as *'If you are to be a leader be patient in your hearing when the petitioner speaks'*. He is said to have had strong ethical principles and sense of moral responsibility, emphasising the importance of social balance, harmony, justice and the collective well-being of the community and promotion of the common good.
3	Ancient Egyptian (North)	Ptahhotep (2375–2350 BCE)	A high official whose philosophy written in *The Maxims of Ptahhotep*, offered guidance on moral conduct, values and ethical decision-making. He stressed the importance of wisdom, respect for authority, humility and social harmony, order and social justice.

			Key themes include the value of listening and patience, the importance of humility and pursuit of self-control. Chapter 4 delves deeper into this.
4	Ethiopian (East)	Zera Yacob (1599–1692)	His work 'Hatata' (Inquiry) made contributions to ideas on rationalism and ethical thought through reasoning. His philosophy is marked by the idea that reason and critical thinking are the foundation of true knowledge and moral understanding. He challenged rigid beliefs and advocated for a rational approach to religion and ethics. His writings reflect a commitment to intellectual integrity and universal principles of justice and human dignity, highlighting the capacity of African and Islamic thought to engage with global philosophical discussions.
5	Ghanaian (West)	Kwame Nkrumah (1909–72) and Kwasi Wiredu (1931–2017)	Both sought to combat colonialism and promote African identity, although their approaches differed. Nkrumah's (Nkrumahism) combined Pan-Africanism, socialism and traditional values, advocating for anti-imperialism, the unification of Africa and economic independence through state control of resources and industrialisation. Wiredu focused on intellectual decolonisation, challenging the alien concepts introduced by colonialism and seeking to revitalise African intellectual traditions by emphasising consensus-based theories of truth and ethical systems rooted in communal values. While Nkrumah emphasised political and economic strategies, Wiredu aimed to restore African philosophical traditions. Both contributed to African self-determination.

Table 2.2 (*Cont.*)

	Country	Philosopher	Core perspective relevant to social work
6	Nigerian (West)	Sophie Bosede Olúwọlé (1935–2018)	The Yoruba philosopher, a key figure in African philosophy, emphasises the wisdom of oral traditions and divination, emphasising the interconnectedness of all beings. She significantly contributes to gender discourse, highlighting women's roles, status and influence in African societies, challenging the notion of African's inherent subjugation.
7	Cameroonian (Central African)	Achille Mbembe (1957–)	From a postcolonial context, Mbembe explores the impact of colonialism on African societies, introducing the concept of 'necropolitics' to describe how sovereign powers determine life and death, highlighting violence and social marginalisation. He argues that colonial legacies manifest in economic exploitation, political oppression and cultural domination. He calls for a rethinking of history and memory, advocating for new forms of solidarity and humanism that challenge oppressive structures and centralise African identities in global discourse.
8	South Africa	Mugabe R M K Z (Rashid) N K Mangena (1924–2019)	Ubuntu, a pre-colonial philosophy, significantly influences community, social and cultural practices. It is a central concept in Southern African thought, promoting mutual respect and interconnectedness. Embodied in the phrase '*I am because we are*' (Mugumbate and Nyanguru, 2015). Mangena's work explores how ubuntu guides ethical practices and social justice, advocating for the integration of traditional African values with modern challenges. He advocates for the restoration of African cultural and moral principles to address contemporary issues in a culturally rooted and forward-thinking manner.

North America

North America consists of 23 countries, including the Caribbean islands, regarded as a sub-region of North America (included in what is called Middle America).

Spotlight on key philosophers and concepts

There are numerous influential philosophical thinkers from North America who have made significant contributions to social work and broader social theory (see Table 2.3). This chapter focuses on a select few who emerged from diverse traditions.

Table 2.3 Key North American (including the Caribbean) philosophers relevant to social work

	Country	**Philosopher**	**Core perspective relevant to social work**
1	America	John Dewey (1859–1952)	Pragmatic philosophy emphasises the importance of practical consequences in real-world situations, guiding the truth and value of ideas. Dewey's ideas, particularly in education, emphasised the direct impact of education on students' lives and the value of experience and experimentation. He believed that education should prepare people for active engagement in democratic society. In social work practice, Dewey's ideas emphasise hands-on, experience-based learning and the need for social workers to take on a learner role, involving service-users in problem-solving processes. See Chapter 4 for more details on this aspect.
2	America	John Rawls (1921–2002)	Advocating and promoting justice as fairness to address social and economic disparities for the most disadvantaged. Provides a framework for social workers to promote laws and procedures that advance social justice, ensuring that those most in need receive the necessary support to reach their full potential.

Table 2.3 (Cont.)

	Country	Philosopher	Core perspective relevant to social work
3	America	Carol Gilligan (1936–)	The philosophy of caring ethics challenges conventional moral development beliefs by highlighting the importance of connections and caring in moral decision-making. It advocates for an ethics of care that values responsiveness and empathy, the importance of developing compassionate relationships with service-users and prioritising their well-being.
4	African America	Huey P Newton (1942–89), Elbert Howard (1938–2018) and Bobby Seale (1936–)	The founders of the Black Panther Party (Revolutionary Activism and Black Liberation) emphasised social justice, community leadership and self-defence, arguing for drastic changes to overcome racism and economic exploitation. The Party's conceptual framework encourages practitioners to confront systemic injustices and give marginalised populations a voice through activism and lobbying, promoting a critical approach to social justice.
5	African America	Angela Davis (1944–)	The author's work focuses on the criminal justice system, gender and race, using a critical theory framework to raise awareness of oppression and promote change. She advocates for social structures for social justice and rehabilitation and dismantling the prison-industrial complex. Her framework emphasises confronting systemic inequalities and promoting transformative justice techniques that prioritise community assistance and healing over punishment. These ideas are further explored in Chapter 4.

6	Canada	John Ralston Saul (1947–)	Known for his works on citizenship, democracy and the importance of the public intellectual. His book *The Comeback: How Aboriginals are Reclaiming Power and Influence* (Saul, 2015) examines the resurgence of Aboriginal peoples and their impact on Canadian culture.
7	African America	Leonard Harris (1948–)	Combining African American social philosophy with traditional American pragmatism, he emphasises emancipation and social transformation. He advocates a philosophical perspective grounded in African Americans' real-world concerns, highlighting the need for culturally appropriate interventions and practical techniques to address racial disparities and foster social change.
8	African America	bell hooks (1952–2021)	Cultural criticism and intersectional feminism are feminist theories that explore the interplay between race, gender and class, promoting an inclusive and revolutionary feminist movement. These philosophies emphasise the value of community and love in bringing about social change. hooks' philosophy supports an intersectional approach, recognising multiple forms of oppression simultaneously. Her writings, such as *Feminist Theory: From Margin to Centre* (hooks, 2010) and *Ain't I a Woman?* (hooks, 2014), have played a crucial role in addressing disadvantaged groups.

→

Table 2.3 (*Cont.*)

	Country	Philosopher	Core perspective relevant to social work
9	African America	Cornel West (1953–)	Uses philosophical frameworks such as social criticism and predictive pragmatism to analyse modern social concerns. He incorporates moral and religious traditions, pragmatism and social justice, stressing the importance of speaking the truth and acting compassionately in social action. It is important that professional power to critically analyse and empower others will address societal inequalities with compassion and moral integrity.
10	Canada	Taiaiake Alfred (1968–) and Leanne Betasamosake Simpson (1971–)	Both are committed to decolonisation, self-determination and Indigenous revival (reclaiming Indigenous governance and cultural revival, challenging colonial systems and advocating for Indigenous autonomy). Alfred, a Kahnawake Mohawk researcher, stresses political resistance tactics, whereas Simpson, an Anishinaabe activist, highlights the preservation of Indigenous customs and civilisations as crucial to the fight against colonisation and for cultural preservation and Indigenous-led initiatives.
11	Trinidad and Tobago	Cyril Lionel Robert James (1901–89)	As a Pan-Africanist and Marxist, he draws attention to the struggles of peoples of the African diaspora and the interplay of race, class and colonialism. Advocates for international cooperation in combating injustice and promoting global solidarity. James' writings, particularly *The Black Jacobins* (James, 2023), highlight the fight against slavery and colonialism, the importance of social movements, resistance and historical context, which has significantly influenced discussions about anti-oppression and empowerment.

| 12 | Martinique (Caribbean) | Frantz Fanon (1925–61) | Examining the psychological effects of colonialism and the journey to liberation for colonised individuals, he contended that colonial tyranny dehumanises both the oppressor and the oppressed. He stressed the significance of understanding the psychological and historical ramifications of oppression, advocating for decolonisation to promote empowerment and healing. His works, *The Wretched of the Earth* (Fanon, 1961) and *Black Skin, White Masks* (Fanon, 2021) have profoundly impacted discourse on identity, freedom, decolonisation, racism and social justice. Refer to Chapter 4 for further insights on this issue. |
| 13 | Jamaica | Stuart Hall (1932–2014) | Investigated the function of ideology in constructing social reality and analysed the impact of culture and media on identities and power dynamics. He developed postcolonial theory and cultural studies to promote a critical examination of cultural representations and their effects on oppressed populations. It is imperative to critically examine cultural narratives and media representations, to enhance comprehension and management of the social difficulties. This topic is further developed in Chapter 4. |

South America

The five primary cultural regions – the Amazon Basin, the Mixed Mestizo Region, the Tropical Plantation Region, the Rural American Region and the European Commercial Region (Southern Cone) – indicate the predominant ethnic groups and economic activities. South America is made up of 12 nations: Bolivia, Peru, Ecuador, Brazil, Colombia, Venezuela, Guyana, Suriname, Argentina, Uruguay, Paraguay and Peru.

Spotlight on key philosophers and concepts

The Andean Indigenous cultures of the Quechua and Aymara peoples in particular, whose worldviews stretch back to pre-Columbian times (predating the fifteenth-century European colonisation of the Americas, which includes the cultures and civilisations that existed before Christopher Columbus's arrival in 1492 and were essential to civilisations like the Inca Empire), are the source of the idea of Buen Vivir. These beliefs place a strong emphasis on spiritual ties, collectivism and coexisting with nature, and have long been ingrained in Andean societies. Although Buen Vivir has roots in the fifteenth and earlier centuries, it was not until the late twentieth and early twenty-first centuries – especially in Ecuador and Bolivia – that this philosophy was formalised and incorporated into modern political and social frameworks. Buen Vivir reflects a way of life that places a premium on sustainability and the well-being of the community and the environment, and social harmony. The Indigenous philosophy provides significant insights for social work practice, especially when it comes to community-based approaches, ecological sustainability and collective well-being.

Below in Table 2.4 are some South American philosophers who have made significant contributions to political theory, social justice and cultural critique, all of which are highly relevant for social work.

Table 2.4 Key South American philosophers relevant to social work

	Country	Philosopher	Core perspective relevant to social work
1	Cuban	José Martí (1853–95)	Promoted justice, equality and human dignity while fighting for Cuba's independence from colonial powers. He focused on the liberation of oppressed peoples and his conception of a just society, with the human rights and social equity tenets of social work aligning.
2	Peru	Luis Alberto Sánchez (1906–94)	Contributed substantially to the understanding of political and socioeconomic issues across Latin America. Illuminated the challenges and prospects of advancing political and social transformation through advocacy for democracy and social reform.

3	Mexican	Leopoldo Zea (1912–2004)	Focused on the philosophical and cultural identity of the continent being studied. Researched the concept of 'Latin American identity', which entailed investigating the consequences of colonisation as well as the process of coming to terms with one's own cultural heritage.
4	Brazilian	Paulo Freire (1921–97)	His influential book *Pedagogy of the Oppressed* (Freire, 1970) revolutionised education by emphasising its role as a tool for emancipation, empowerment and social change. Stressed the importance of students engaging with oppressive systems, critically engaging with the outside world and actively participating in their education and freedom, particularly in community development and empowerment. Freire's views on dialogue, critical consciousness and the intersection of theory and action have significantly impacted social work practice. He emphasised the value of challenging conventional wisdom and encouraging inclusive practices to build stronger communities and individuals, offering a framework for advancing social justice, equality and revolutionary change.

Europe

There are 50 countries in Europe, but only 44 of them have their capital city on the European continent. Europe is divided into several regions and peninsulas. Western Europe includes nations such as Germany, France, Spain, Portugal, Belgium, the Netherlands, Luxembourg, Switzerland, and Austria. Northern Europe encompasses the United Kingdom, Ireland, Denmark, Norway, Sweden, Finland and Iceland. Southern Europe comprises Italy, Greece, Spain, Portugal, Malta and Cyprus. Eastern Europe comprises countries like Russia, Poland, the Czech Republic, Hungary, Romania, Bulgaria, Slovakia, Estonia, Latvia and Lithuania.

Spotlight on key philosophers and concepts

European philosophical traditions as outlined in Table 2.5 below have diverse perspectives on morality, ethics and religion, ranging from ancient to modern ethical theories. Values such as individual autonomy, justice and rationality are relevant for social work practice; these philosophies contribute to discussions on human rights, ethical dilemmas and the importance of autonomy and justice in interventions.

Ancient philosophy

Ideas from ancient philosophy have had a significant impact on Western thought, which is still relevant in the discussion of ethics today. These philosophers emphasised concepts such as virtue, justice and the good life – which continue to inform the social work profession's approach to social justice and human well-being.

Table 2.5 Key European philosophers relevant to social work

	Country	Philosopher	Core perspective relevant to social work
1	Greece	Socrates (469–399 BCE)	The Socratic method, a dialectical questioning technique, promotes knowledge and moral virtue. It encourages self-awareness and clarity through cooperative argumentative dialogue, stimulating critical thinking and illuminating ideas through open-ended questions that encourage deep exploration of thoughts and beliefs. This topic is developed further in Chapter 4.
2	Greece	Plato (427–347 BCE)	Socrates' pupil focused on the significance of reason, justice and reason's role in creating a just society. His views on the ideals of justice and goodness are consistent with moral behaviour and social justice.
3	Greece	Aristotle (384–322 BCE)	A pupil of Plato who stressed the natural world and making empirical observations. The golden mean theory, with a focus on phronesis, or practical wisdom, promoting harmony between extremes, is evident in social work's emphasis on moral decision-making and the promotion of well-being.

| 4 | Greece | Hippocrates (460–370 BCE) | The 'Father of Medicine' popularised the notion that illness has natural causes and needs to be treated with compassion and care. His moral philosophy of medicine – especially the Hippocratic Oath of 'do no harm' – highlights respect for people's worth and dignity. |

Modern philosophy

Modern perspectives on individual rights, ethics and the structure of society were brought to ethical and social thought by modern philosophy. The ideas of human rights, autonomy and evidence-based practice that underpin social work today were profoundly shaped by these philosophers (see Table 2.6).

Table 2.6 Key European philosophers relevant to social work

	Country	**Philosopher**	**Core perspective relevant to social work**
1	France	René Descartes (1596–1650)	Well-known for focusing on doubt and reason, he made a key contribution to the creation of dualism, the concept that the mind and the body are two distinct things. Descartes placed a strong emphasis on the importance of challenging presumptions and advocated ongoing assessment and reassessment of his approaches to ensure interventions were effective.
2	England	John Locke (1632–1704)	A key figure in liberal political philosophy, promoting the idea of natural rights, such as life, liberty and property, he placed a strong emphasis on the social contract and empirical data. His views on the social contract and natural rights serve as the foundation for many ethical precepts, including support of service-users' rights and regard for their autonomy. See Chapter 4 for more details.

Table 2.6 (Cont.)

	Country	Philosopher	Core perspective relevant to social work
3	Prussia	Immanuel Kant (1724–1804)	Deontological ethics emphasises responsibility and moral law, which have affected ethical theories. He asserted that decisions and acts must be morally justified and guided by universal principles. This aligns with a commitment to treating everyone with dignity and respect.
4	Scotland	David Hume (1711–76)	Empiricism is supported by and emphasises information gained from sensory experience. It additionally encourages the use of evidence-based practice. Hume's philosophy advocates that practitioners should ground their actions and policy decisions in empirical facts and observable evidence. Moral judgements arise not solely from reason, but from our emotional responses to actions and character traits. This topic is further developed in Chapter 4.
5	Germany	Georg Wilhelm Friedrich Hegel (1770–1831)	A key figure in idealism, his theories on the dialectical process, which reconciles opposing viewpoints (thesis and antithesis) to produce a fresh understanding (synthesis), are consistent with resolving disputes and bringing about change. He frequently mediates between divergent points of view, which is an application of Hegelian dialectics.
6	England	John Stuart Mill (1806–73)	The utilitarian philosophy promotes deeds that maximise happiness and well-being for the greatest number of people. Emphasising empowerment and social justice advocacy is in line with Mill's emphasis on liberty, freedom of expression and individual rights.

Postmodern philosophy

Critical analysis of power dynamics and identity-formation has had a significant influence on social work. For social workers dealing with issues of inequality and marginalisation, these philosophers offer insights into the complexities of human existence, social institutions and the dynamics of oppression and resistance (see Table 2.7). In particular, existentialists believe every human being is a free, responsible agent who shapes their own destiny via volitional actions.

Table 2.7 Key European philosophers relevant to social work

	Country	Philosopher	Core perspective relevant to social work
1	Germany	Friedrich Nietzsche (1844–1900)	Challenged traditional morality and advocated for the concept of the Übermensch, focusing on cultivating individual ideals and personal growth. His worldview encourages resilience and empowerment, challenging individuals to live fully and truly.
2	Germany	Hannah Arendt (1906–75)	Researched authority, power and totalitarianism to offer insights on civic engagement and the nature of power. Arendt's work informs social work's focus on community organising, advocacy and democratic participation.
3	France	Simone de Beauvoir (1908–86)	The topics of gender, identity and oppression were studied by this renowned existentialist and feminist philosopher. Her work is about commitment to empowering women and marginalised groups, promoting gender equality.
4	Algeria	Jacques Derrida (1930–2004)	The concept of deconstruction stresses language's fluidity and questions fixed meanings to comprehend the various narratives that service-users have to tell. Derrida's theory is in favour of a more comprehensive and nuanced strategy, in which intervention tactics centre on the complexity of service-users' experiences.

Oceania/Australasia

Oceania is divided into four regions: Melanesia, Micronesia, Polynesia and Australasia (Australia and New Zealand). Oceania is made up of 14 countries, many extremely small. Given that it comprises the entire continent, Australia is the only nation that possesses both continental and national status. Nonetheless, due to their many similarities, New Zealand, which is its neighbour and a member of Oceania, is included in this section of the chapter.

Spotlight on key philosophers and concepts

Table 2.8 highlights the Indigenous Australian knowledge, educational practices and community well-being are significantly influenced by the Aboriginal Australian concept of the Dreaming, which promotes environmental stewardship and shared obligations. Indigenous kinship systems emphasise interconnectedness, storytelling and oral traditions, while the concept of Two-Spirit Identity promotes inclusivity. New Zealand's Māori philosophy emphasises community well-being, respect for ancestors and connection to nature. Modern social work practices prioritise social justice and cultural humility, treating marginalised groups with dignity and compassion. Western philosophical contributions to the utilitarian approach inform ethical decision-making and advocacy, emphasising the alleviation of suffering and the advancement of social welfare. These perspectives, combined with the decolonisation, Indigenous sovereignty and self-determination, contribute to a more inclusive and respectful social work environment.

Table 2.8 Key Oceanian and Australasian philosophers relevant to social work

	Country	Philosopher	Core perspective relevant to social work
1	Australian (Aboriginal)	Uncle Bob Randall (1934–2015)	Highlights the moral and spiritual aspects of Indigenous life, emphasising the value of preserving cultural practices and knowledge by focusing on the relationship between land, community and oral traditions. By promoting Indigenous values and traditions, this viewpoint enhances social work.

2	Tonga	Epeli Hau'ofa (1939–2009)	Renowned for his contributions to postcolonial and Pacific studies, he advocated for cultural acceptance and respect through his critique of colonial narratives. His emphasis is on the cultural strength of Pacific Islanders. In addition to highlighting the resiliency and agency of Pacific Islander cultures, his work questions colonial presumptions.
3	Australia	Peter Singer (1946–)	An established authority in applied ethics and bioethics, Singer takes a utilitarian stance that prioritises lessening suffering and advancing social welfare.
4	Australian (Aboriginal)	Chris Sarra (1964–)	Recognised for his contributions to social justice and education, Sarra advocates for Aboriginal identities and educational approaches that preserve and promote Indigenous values, highlighting the need for equitable and culturally sensitive educational reforms.

Psychological concepts

Psychological concepts include the conscious and unconscious, projection identification and thinking. Freud's (1899, 1901) concept of the unconscious/conscious refers to desires, feelings, memories and thoughts that are outside of conscious awareness but nevertheless influence individual behaviour and experiences. According to Freud, the unconscious mind contains forgotten or repressed emotions, thoughts and inclinations that stem from early childhood experiences or conflicts. These unconscious elements can impact a person's behaviours, dreams and thoughts, often manifesting in subtle ways, such as slips of the tongue (known as a Freudian slip). Freud believed exploring and understanding the unconscious were crucial in uncovering the root causes of psychological issues and behaviour.

People have complex histories and views. The research on which this guide is based demonstrates how people deal with these histories and views. Some, for example, are completely unaware of how their biography impacts their professional life, while others – who are more aware – attempt to leave their personal views behind when they go to work. Both approaches can create problems. Being unaware of your biography, for example, can result in bias. However, Weekes' (2020) study showed that those who try to set their history aside in a work environment can sometimes adopt an arid professional stance, negating the richness of the experience they could bring to their relational and emotive role. It is clear from these findings that people need to own their individual complexities, because these complexities, consciously or unconsciously, impact on their role and function. Only by taking ownership of our personal history can we make positive use of it in our decision-making. The starting point is to understand the connection between our early experiences and our adult sense of self.

It was psychoanalyst Melanie Klein who, in the 1920s, first recognised the importance of our earliest childhood experiences in the formation of our adult emotional world. Following the work of Sigmund Freud, Klein (1975) proposed that the essential sense of self is determined through a process of 'splitting'. This is the tendency of a (pre-verbal) infant to unconsciously separate objects, and the sense of self, into good and bad parts. This is due to not having a mechanism to manage the conflicting fantasies, so endeavouring to survive. However, as the infant is unable to maintain a unified mental image of an object as both good and bad, they will often project the negative aspects of their mental state onto an external object (the mother). This is the basis of a concept known as projective identification (Klein, 2012), a defence mechanism against both good and bad aspects of the self – the processes by which the self is split off and projected into an object.

Wilfred Bion (1962) extended Klein's work, proposing that the infant's early experiences with its mother form the foundations of later processes in relation to mental states and thinking. Bion's concept of thinking encompasses the capacity to contain and process emotional experience. Bion regarded thinking as an innate function, a process of integrating and understanding emotional and sensory experiences. Based on this, Bion (1988) developed his ideas into a model of thought classification, which stems from the relationship between the baby and the mother. It was these ideas that led Bion to the conclusion that an individual's competence and skill development are related to early emotional experiences. The essential component for thinking is the link between emotion and expression. The concept also includes the idea of 'thoughts without a thinker' – the concept that thoughts exist independently of whether an individual recognises them (unconscious) or is able to articulate them. Bion was concerned with an individual's ability to tolerate the unknown and the unprocessed thought, leading to the development of deeper insights, understanding and personal growth.

These ideas are fundamental to the concept of bias. This is a topic that has been the subject of considerable discussion over recent years, and much has been written about it. Less well covered, however, is the subject of how to deal with its effects, particularly within a professional environment. While the existence of bias is increasingly recognised, the extent to which organisations offer advice and guidance on how employees and workers can recognise and manage it can be limited. Often, they are merely urged to be aware of bias and to do what they can to limit its effects on their thinking and decision-making. Rarely is a defined methodology, based on evidence, suggested to help people take active steps to improving their decision-making and judgements.

Sociology frameworks

Finally, sociological research often involves a combination of these perspectives and theories to analyse complex social phenomena and societal causality. The concept of societal causality seeks to explore and understand the cause-and-effect relationships that exist within society by examining how factors, such as individual behaviours, cultural norms and social structures/institutions contribute to specific outcomes or patterns within a given society. In this chapter, sociological theories are addressed with reference to equitability. In the United Kingdom, this is the *Equality Act 2010*; as mentioned above, many other countries have similar legal instruments. The United Kingdom has nine protected characteristics, which are enshrined in law protection for individuals; this chapter adds a tenth, given the universally accepted recognition that an individual's social class has a significant impact on life experiences and chances, even if it is not protected by legislation.

Age

Understanding the experiences of different age groups and addressing age-related diversity is crucial for promoting inclusivity and ensuring the recognition of rights for individuals of all ages. Ageism is discrimination based upon an individual's age, which shapes perceptions and treatment for all in distinct ways.

Concerning the young, it manifests in assumptions of inexperience, immaturity or lack of knowledge, often hindering opportunities in academic and professional environments. Such discrimination is based solely on age, so older people are overlooked despite skills and experience, often leading to frustration, demotivation and a sense of being undervalued. Assumptions about declining abilities, resistance to change or technological ineptitude are made about older individuals, resulting in elders feeling excluded and isolated, and reinforcing a sense of obsolescence and being excluded from job opportunities or social activities.

Researchers have equally found that the young are also overlooked in that there is limited research on the experiences of young people (Bratt et al, 2020; de la Fuente-Núñez et al, 2021). Both ends of the age continuum can often experience prejudice, which perpetuates a cycle of discrimination and limits the potential contributions both older and younger people can make to society.

The theoretical focus of this chapter highlights that of elders, due to the fact that *'there is currently no coherent theory on ageism as it affects younger populations'* (de la Fuente-Núñez et al, 2021, p 13). Cumming and Henry (1961) suggested that individuals naturally withdraw from social roles and relationships as they age. According to their disengagement theory, older adults disengage from work and community involvement, leading to decreased recognition and potential marginalisation. Activity theory suggests that for individuals across the age spectrum to be healthy and have positive well-being, they should maintain an active engagement in activities, hobbies and social roles (Havighurst, 1961). To foster an inclusive society and challenge ageist assumptions that may limit rights and opportunities, respect for everyone's abilities and skills is required.

By exploring disengagement and activity theories in relation to age, social workers can develop an understanding of the challenges faced by the various age groups. This is essential for creating inclusive communities, policies and services to empower individuals across the lifespan.

Class

Grasping the significance of social class from a sociological perspective is crucial for addressing issues of equality. While not addressed by equality legislation, socio-economic inequalities permeate society, reflected in poverty and homelessness. An examination of how social class shapes experiences and opportunities enables the identification of systemic barriers and disparities that contribute to inequality. An understanding of it assists in advocating for the promotion of social justice and equitable resource distribution to address the impact on individuals and communities.

Several sociological theories offer useful perspectives on social class, including those of Karl Marx (1848), Emile Durkheim's (1884) conflict theory, Talcott Parsons' (1951) structural functionalism and Max Weber's (1968) interpretive sociology. Marx viewed social class as a source of conflict and a catalyst for social change, arguing that social class divisions are rooted in the unequal distribution of power, wealth and resources. According to conflict theory, the capitalist system perpetuates social inequalities by exploiting labour for economic gain, highlighting the inherent conflict between the capitalist class (bourgeoisie) and the working class (proletariat). Social class struggles drive social change as oppressed classes challenge and seek to transform the existing class structure, advocating for the need to address power imbalances and create a more equitable society.

In contrast, structural functionalists such as Durkheim and Parsons view social class as a social structure that performs the essential function for society of maintaining systems of equilibrium and social cohesion by assigning different positions based on abilities, qualifications and skills, leading to inevitable social inequality. However, this perspective emphasises the positive contributions of social class to social order and stability, highlighting the shared values and norms that bind individuals within a given class structure.

Conversely, Weber's interpretive sociology centres on understanding social actors' motives and the context in which they act through the subjective meanings they attach to their actions. He defines class as comprising three elements: the economic basis (property ownership and an individual's market situation, including skills, qualifications and opportunities); status (the honour and social esteem of individuals or groups); and party (organised groups' ability to advocate, influence social action and access power).

These contrasting perspectives provide valuable insights into social stratification, with structural functionalism focusing on the role of social class in maintaining social order while conflict theory emphasises the conflicts and power struggles arising from class divisions. Interpretive sociology views class as a multi-dimensional concept encompassing economic position, social status and political influence. Understanding such perspectives allows for a comprehensive analysis of the complexities surrounding social class and the pursuit of greater equality within society.

Disability (physical or mental)

Sociological theories reveal that disability is not merely a medical or individual issue, but socially constructed. They provide a framework to examine how societal structures impact the experiences and treatment of disabled individuals, highlighting that the social construction of disability, societal barriers and systemic factors rather than their impairments contribute to the discrimination and marginalisation of disabled people.

Hippocrates (c. 460–370 BCE) and Galen (129–c. 216 CE) shaped what is referred to as the medical model of disability by focusing on the biological and physiological aspects of health and illness. Hippocrates introduced the idea of natural causes for diseases and went on to undertake detailed anatomical studies, thus viewing disability as a medical condition requiring diagnosis and treatment.

Howard Becker (1928-23) highlighted the role of social interactions and the labels assigned to individuals in shaping their self-perception and how others treat them. When Becker's (1963) labelling theory is applied to disability, people with disabilities are not seen as inherently different; rather, their experiences and opportunities are influenced by societal labels, which often generate stereotypes, misconceptions and assumptions about them. This leads to social exclusion, marginalisation and unequal treatment that all shape disability identities and perpetuate inequality. The labels attached to individuals with disabilities can shape their sense of self, limit their opportunities and affect their interactions with others (Link and Phelan, 2001).

In contrast, Oliver (1990) explores the social model of disability, arguing that disability arises from societal attitudes and barriers, and it is these rather than the impairments themselves that serve to disadvantage and exclude people. This model shifts the focus from the individual's physical or mental limitations to the societal and environmental obstacles that prevent full participation and inclusion.

Gender reassignment (both undergoing or undergone)

Examining gender reassignment through the lens of theory assists the comprehension of the complex social dynamics and personal experiences involved in transitioning. These theoretical frameworks help to illuminate the social, cultural and political factors that influence gender identity, and the ways societal norms and expectations shape individuals' experiences of gender reassignment and the challenges they face.

Following the AIDS crisis, queer theory emerged in the United States in the 1990s as a transformative framework within sociology, challenging conventional notions of gender and sexuality. The theory put forward the idea that gender and sexual identities are complex and fluid. Central to queer theory is an assertion that gender is not solely determined by biological sex, but encompasses a spectrum of identities, expressions and experiences. Queer theory critiques the societal norms surrounding gender roles and expressions, encouraging the celebration of diverse gender expressions and dismantling rigid gender norms (Halberstam, 1998). It offers a challenge to the fixed and traditional categories of male and female, offering alternative frameworks that encompass diverse gender identities such as non-binary, genderqueer and genderfluid (Butler, 1990), stressing the importance of respecting self-identified gender identity and recognising the validity of gender reassignment processes (Lev, 2004). Queer theory further highlights that, like everyone, transgendered individuals hold several identities that expose them to various forms of oppression, including classism and racism (Stryker and Whittle, 2006). By embracing and understanding all aspects of their uniqueness, society has the potential to cultivate inclusivity and acceptance.

Marriage and civil partnership status

Sociological perspectives such as functionalism, symbolic interactionism and postmodern theory provide critical insight and understanding into the complexities of marriage and civil partnership status, particularly how these institutions function and are shaped by and reflect broader social and societal structures, norms and changes. Marriage and civil partnerships are social institutions that have evolved over time, influenced by functionalism and postmodern theory.

Functionalism, as proposed by Durkheim (1997) and Parsons (1951), views marriage as essential for maintaining and sustaining societal order (social stability and cohesion) by regulating relationships, reproducing social norms and integrating individuals into society. Functionalist theorists emphasise the roles of marriage and civil partnerships in procreation, socialising children, regulating sexual behaviour and creating a division of labour within households to enhance efficiency and reinforce social norms and values. Conversely, symbolic interactionism focuses on how individuals interpret, experience and negotiate their identities and roles within the social construct of marriage and civil partnerships, emphasising the personal meanings and social interactions that shape these relationships. This perspective provides insights into the dynamic nature of marriage and civil partnerships, balancing their role in societal stability with the changing social and individual factors.

Equally, postmodern theory highlights the evolving and fluid nature of marriage and civil partnerships in contemporary society (Beck and Beck-Gernsheim, 2001; Giddens, 1992). Postmodern theorists argue that these institutions are shaped by individual choices, personal preferences and the pursuit of personal fulfilment. This perspective points to the impact of increased gender equality, reflecting the impact of greater gender equality, shifting social norms, and the recognition of diverse sexual orientations, and other forms of partnerships such as same-sex marriages and non-traditional family structures (Giddens, 1992).

Pregnancy and maternity

Applying sociological theories is essential for understanding maternity and pregnancy as they offer insights into how social structures, norms and values shape experiences and expectations surrounding these aspects of life.

Pregnancy and maternity are transformative experiences shaped by social interactions and pregnancy-related symbols and language, such as 'motherhood' and 'baby bump', which carry cultural meanings that shape perceptions and behaviours. Symbolic interactionism recognises the socially constructed phenomena of pregnancy and maternity influenced by cultural beliefs, norms and expectations. It emphasises how individuals and societies construct meanings and negotiate pregnancy and motherhood, focusing on the personal and cultural communication and interpretations that influence experiences. These theories help reveal how societal expectations, family members, friends, healthcare systems, wider society and cultural practices impact the experiences of pregnant individuals and new parents, offering a deeper understanding of the intersection between personal identity and societal expectations.

The theory emphasises the intersections of gender, reproductive rights and work–life balance, shedding light on the challenges and inequalities experienced by pregnant individuals and parents. Applying symbolic interactionism enhances the understanding of the complex social dynamics of pregnancy and maternity, navigating towards strategies that promote inclusivity and equitability for those affected.

Race (inclusive of colour, ethnicity, national origin)

The application of sociological theories such as critical race theory, postcolonialism and conflict theory provides valuable perspectives to reveal how race as a social construct leads to racial inequalities, and how racism is constructed and perpetuated.

Conflict theory examines the ongoing conflicts and power struggles between different socially constructed racial groups, focusing on power, resources and inequalities (Marx, 1848). It stresses how economic and social inequalities drive racial tensions and discrimination. Conflict theory explores how dominant racial and ethnic groups maintain privilege and control over resources, perpetuating discrimination and the marginalisation of minority groups. This theory emphasises the role of social structures and institutions in maintaining inequalities through systemic oppression, such as institutional racism. Conflict theory highlights the importance of collective actions and advocacy in challenging oppressive systems and promoting social change.

Postcolonial theory examines the enduring effects of colonialism on individuals and racial, societal dynamics (Said, 1978), exposing how historical power imbalances continue to shape contemporary racial issues and identities. It analyses power dynamics between colonisers and the colonised, exploring how colonial histories shape contemporary social, cultural and economic structures. Postcolonial theory provides insights into how dominant cultures continue to marginalise formerly colonised populations, perpetuating racial inequalities. It explores the resistance and agency of marginalised communities in challenging colonial narratives and structures, contributing to decolonisation and social justice (Fanon, 1961).

Critical race theory (CRT) explores how racism is embedded and ingrained within social systems, structures and institutions, highlighting privilege and disadvantage and how these racial inequalities impact marginalised racial groups (Delgado and Stefancic, 2001). CRT challenges the notion of race as a biological trait, focusing instead on how race intersects with other identities, such as gender and class, to create unique experiences of discrimination (Crenshaw, 1989). CRT facilitates an analysis of systemic racism and develops strategies to dismantle these structures, promoting racial equality and social justice.

Together, these three theories offer a comprehensive framework for analysing and addressing the multifaceted nature of racism and the systemic factors that perpetuate racial inequalities.

Religion or belief (non-belief)

Oxhandler et al (2015) note that despite the recognition of religion and spirituality as important aspects of service-users' culture practice, negativity still exists regarding these topics in the social work education. Social work educators who are possibly not trained on how to discuss service-users' religion and spirituality, or who hold strong negative views about these topics, often discourage students from bringing them up. This sends a clear message to students, who then enter practice ill-prepared to address these issues when clients raise them. Religion has been extensively analysed within sociology, with scholars offering diverse perspectives on its role and significance. Foundational and valuable insights into the area of religion have been greatly enhanced by three influential sociologists, Karl Marx, Max Weber and Émile Durkheim, who provided distinct viewpoints on religion, shedding light on its functions, social implications and relationship with societal structures.

Marx (1848) approached religion critically, considering it an instrument of social control and a product of the social and economic conditions of capitalism. He famously referred to religion as the 'opium of the people', suggesting it acts to pacify the working class and reflect societal inequalities. Marx viewed the control exerted by religion as used by the ruling class to maintain power and perpetuate economic inequalities.

In contrast, Weber (2002) took a nuanced approach, focusing on the relationship between religion and social change. He emphasised the role of religious beliefs and values, particularly how religious ethics such as the Protestant work ethic steered economic and social behaviour, contributing to the development and rise of capitalism with its associated Protestant values.

Lastly, Durkheim's (1997) theory emphasises religion as a social phenomenon promoting social cohesion, solidarity and collective consciousness of religious practices. He believed religion creates and reinforces social bonds, shared values and moral order within a community, providing a sense of belonging and cohesion among its adherents and acting as a crucial element in maintaining social order.

Together, these theories highlight the complex and multifaceted ways in which religion functions, influences and is influenced by social structures, power dynamics and economic systems, and the social implications and resultant change.

Sex (gender)

Before exploring the theories in this section, it is important to define the terms 'gender' and 'sex', as they are often viewed as the same whereas they are in fact distinctly different. Gender is socially constructed and establishes hierarchies and inequalities that intersect with other social and economic disparities. It refers to socially constructed roles, behaviours, expressions and identities of girls, women, boys, men and gender-diverse people, where the binary is arguably neither confined nor fixed. Ideas of gender shape and influence self-perception, interactions and the distribution of power and resources in society. Significant diversity and complexity exist in how people experience and express gender through their roles, expectations, relationships and societal institutions. Sex pertains to the collection of biological characteristics, predominantly encompassing physical and physiological traits such as chromosomes, gene expression, hormone levels and functions, as well as reproductive and sexual anatomy. While sex is commonly classified as female or male, there exists variability in the biological attributes that constitute sex and their expression.

Pivotal to understanding gender issues is a sociological framework that illuminates how social structures and cultural beliefs shape these experiences. Symbolic interactionism in the context of gender views gender as a social construct that is continuously created and negotiated through interpersonal interactions (West and Zimmerman, 1987), highlighting how individuals interpret their social world through everyday interactions, language and symbols (Blumer, 1986). This perspective stresses the fluidity of gender, which is shaped by societal norms and expectations. By examining these interactions, symbolic interactionism helps us understand how gender roles and stereotypes are constructed and perpetuated, influencing self-perception and identity-formation.

Additionally, feminist and womanist theories contribute to understanding women's experiences and gender inequality. While both strive for gender equality, they differ in terms of their contextual and cultural lenses. Feminism focuses on the social, political and economic equality disparities of women, challenging patriarchal norms and advocating for women's rights. In contrast, womanism (Collins, 1996) expands the feminist discourse to include the unique oppression faced by Black woman, recognising and emphasising the interconnectedness of gender, race and class.

Sexual orientation

Queer theory challenges traditional understandings of gender, sexuality and identity, offering a lens to explore the experiences of transgendered individuals in their pursuit of diversity and equality (Butler, 1990; Halberstam, 1998). It rejects fixed, binary categories of gender and sexuality, recognising the fluidity and complexity of human identities. The theory seeks to dismantle societal norms that marginalise those who do not conform to traditional gender and sexual norms (Rubin, 2012; Sedgwick, 1990). Queer theory highlights the importance of acknowledging and affirming the diverse gender identities beyond the male–female binary and challenges the notion that gender is solely determined by biological sex (Butler, 1990; Halberstam, 1998).

Queer theory critiques the assumptions of cisnormativity, namely that cisgender identities are the norm, stressing that these assumptions marginalise transgender individuals and perpetuate inequality (Butler, 1990; Halberstam, 1998). The theory seeks to challenge oppressive systems, advocating for transgender rights and social change (Spade, 2015; Stryker and Whittle, 2006). Additionally, queer theory seeks to illuminate the fact that transgendered individuals also have other identities based on their race, class and disability, and thus may be subject to multiple forms of oppression (Stryker and Whittle, 2006). By embracing queer theory, society can become more inclusive for all individuals, irrespective of gender identity or expression.

This all illustrates that social work is based on a respect for the inherent worth and dignity of all people, as expressed in the United Nations Universal Declaration of Human Rights (United Nations, 1948), other related UN declarations and the European Convention on Human Rights and the conventions derived from those declarations.

The purpose of EPPJ, and the associated tool, is to assist individuals to recognise how individuals can unconsciously project the good and bad aspects of themselves onto those who appear in front of them. Based on recent research (see Chapter 1), EPPJ provides a way to improve the decision-making process by helping professionals recognise and understand their own individual biases, and to use them constructively in carrying out their professional role.

Below are two reflective exercises. Choose whether you would like to explore an issue relating to adults or children and families – obviously you are free to do both.

Case study

Navigating adult social work ethical challenges

Alex is the designated social worker for the Williams family, which includes Mr and Mrs Williams, both in their late seventies, and their daughter, Sarah, who is their primary caregiver. Mr Williams has been diagnosed with a terminal illness and the family is navigating complex decisions concerning his care, autonomy and family dynamics.

A key issue is balancing Mr Williams' right to make decisions about his own care with concerns about his mental capacity due to his illness. This challenge involves applying the principles of African communitarianism, which emphasise the interconnectedness of family decisions, and contrasting this with John Locke's perspective on individual rights and autonomy, which prioritises personal decision-making.

Another challenge is navigating cultural perspectives on end-of-life decisions and ensuring the family's wishes align with ethical principles.

Reflective exercise

» Identify three ethical dilemmas you might struggle with personally, clearly explaining what they are and why.

» Address the answer with reference to a comparison of *two* philosophical approaches or *two* philosophers mentioned in the chapter from *two* continents other than your own continent of origin.

» What might be the role of the social worker practising in the United Kingdom, given the influence of *one* European modern or ancient philosopher/philosophical approach?

Case study

Navigating a children and families social work ethical challenge

The Wang family comprises Mr and Mrs Wang, an elderly couple, and their two grandchildren, aged seven and ten, who have been temporarily removed from their parents' care due to emotional abuse and issues related to the parents' mental health. Social worker Fredrick has been assigned to determine the best course of action for the children's well-being, while Jamal, the probation officer, is involved because of the mother's criminal damage to a local supermarket's front door. Finally, the family has experienced historical trauma that may affect individuals.

One of the primary challenges is balancing the parents' rights to make decisions for their children with the need to protect the children from harm. Another significant challenge is determining the best living arrangement for the children while considering their cultural needs and ensuring their safety and well-being.

Addressing the cultural differences that impact communication and understanding within the King/Wang family is also crucial. Additionally, there are systemic issues that contribute to the family's difficulties and advocating for fair treatment is essential.

Reflective exercise

» Identify three ethical dilemmas that, as a social worker, you might struggle with personally, clearly explaining what they are and why.

» Address the answer with reference to a comparison of two philosophical approaches or two philosophers mentioned in the chapter from two continents other than your own continent of origin.

» What might be the role of the social worker practising in the United Kingdom, given the influence of one European modern or ancient philosopher/philosophical approach?

Chapter summary

To answer the question posed at the start of the chapter, a foundational understanding of philosophy, psychology and sociology enriches social work practice by enhancing critical thinking and ethical decision-making and providing a deeper appreciation of the theoretical underpinnings that shape social issues. This understanding allows practitioners and students to engage more effectively in complex social contexts.

Philosophy equips social work practitioners and students with crucial tools for ethical decision-making, deepening understanding of power dynamics, social structures and justice issues and informing ethical practice. Critical thinking enhances individuals' ability to evaluate different perspectives, challenge assumptions and critically appraise interventions and policies, and build conceptual clarity. Finally, philosophical concepts significantly develop anti-discriminatory and empowering social work practice.

Knowledge of psychological theories and principles promotes an understanding of the underlying factors influencing clients' behaviours and experiences. Psychology is fundamental to social work, offering insights into human behaviour, mental health and interpersonal dynamics. Attachment theory, cognitive-behavioural approaches, trauma-informed interventions and reflection are a few of the pillars of relationship-based social work practice that help with the process of empowering service-users.

Finally, sociology provides social workers with a broader understanding of societal structures, power dynamics and social inequalities. This emphasises the importance of social context in shaping group and individual experiences and identities, alongside an appreciation of the systemic and structural factors – all of which are central to addressing oppression and promoting empowerment.

Today, the challenge of meeting the needs of service-users is harder than ever due to increasingly varied populations and society. Service-users and social workers can often have different conscious and unconscious perspectives. Teaching institutions need to meet this challenge by adapting courses to stretch students beyond the practical skills of social work to a deeper, more intellectual understanding of the profession. This arguably must include the study of philosophy, psychology and sociology in social work courses, going beyond a general overview of Eurocentric values and ethics.

Key takeaways from the chapter

- Understanding key philosophical, psychological and sociological concepts ensures the decolonisation of educational curricula and practice and is important to becoming an effective social worker.
- Being self-aware about personal and professional values in relation to others improves the effectiveness of a social worker's role.
- Ethical decision-making, professional behaviour and conduct are guided by an adherence to the Code of Ethics, relevant laws, regulations and appropriate ethical models.
- Social work emphasises the dignity and worth of individuals, upholding principles of social justice and human rights as essential frameworks for emphasising the need for equity in society.

Chapter 3 | Exploring faith and identity: how different religions shape values and behaviour

I respect people of all religions, all faiths…
   Former Australian Prime Minister Scott Morrison (2018)

This chapter seeks to provide the reader with an overview of a selection of world faiths and religions, with the aim of exploring how the two inform the values, actions and behaviours of both social workers and service-users.

Faith, defined as *'confidence and trust in a person'* or *'belief that is not based on proof,'* (Hebrews 11:1) frequently comes first on an individual level, as people typically experience a personal belief or spiritual sense before seeking out or adhering to an organised religion. However, historically and societally, religion – the practice of religious beliefs, ritual observance of faith – can precede individual faith by providing established systems and communities where faith can be nurtured and expressed. Religious people focus on rules, rituals and laws, attending a place of worship, daily reading and reciting verses from a holy book and seeking to attend a pilgrimage. Consequently, while personal faith might initially emerge independently, organised religions have historically structured and guided that faith, making the relationship between the two interdependent and context-dependent, represented by Figure 3.1.

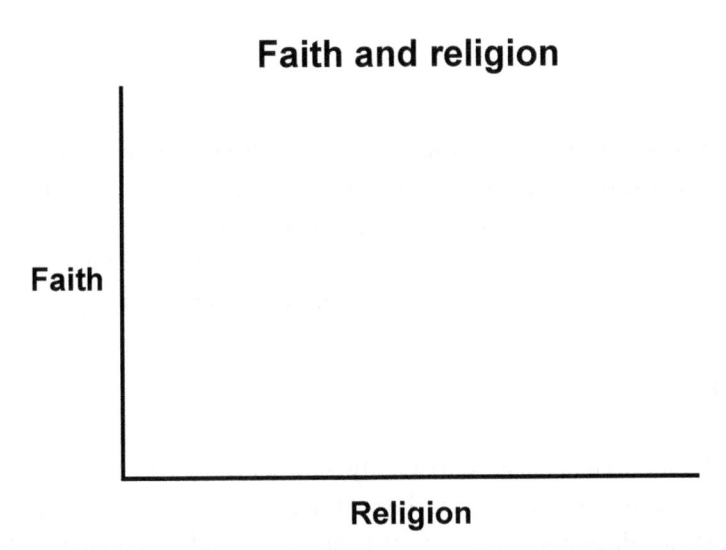

Figure 3.1 Faith and religion axis
Source: Gledhill (2021).

Those who have faith have an inner confidence in the power and protection of God, due to a deep and personal relationship with the divine. They desire to pray and worship God every day and in every way, sharing their faith and holding a sure hope of the afterlife.

Understanding the major world religions depicted in Figure 3.2 is also crucial.

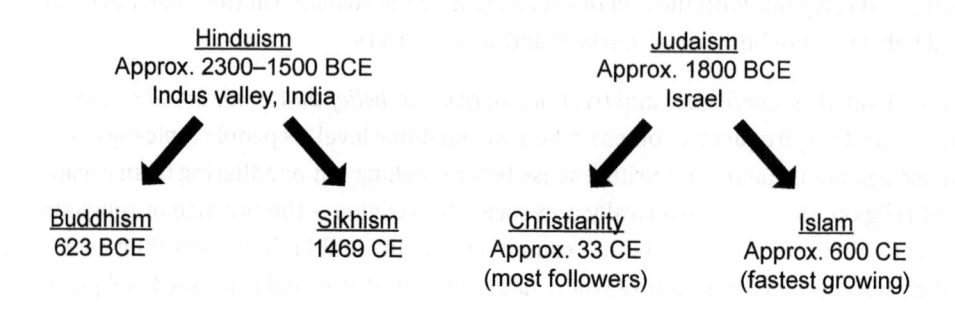

Timeline of religion

Hinduism
Approx. 2300–1500 BCE
Indus valley, India

↙ ↘

Buddhism
623 BCE

Sikhism
1469 CE

Judaism
Approx. 1800 BCE
Israel

↙ ↘

Christianity
Approx. 33 CE
(most followers)

Islam
Approx. 600 CE
(fastest growing)

Note:
BCE = Before Common Era (aka BC, Before Christ)   CE = Common Era (aka AD, Anno Domini, year of the Lord)

Figure 3.2 Timeline of religion

Asia

Asia has a tapestry of diverse faiths and religions, each woven into the cultural and historical fabric of the continent. Ancient original religions such as Hinduism, Buddhism, Islam and Sikhism have influenced the lives, philosophies (see previous chapter) and social structures of millions. The ancient belief systems, ranging from the monotheism of Islam to the polytheism of Hinduism, now coexist with newer religions.

Africa

Due to the legacy of colonialism, Christianity is recognised as the dominant religion in many African countries, and Africa is the continent with the largest observance of the various Christian denominations. However, there are significant numbers of Muslims, alongside those who adhere to the traditional African religions, interspersed throughout the different regions. Nigeria and Ghana have significant Islamic sectors. South Africa and Zimbabwe are mainly Christian, with Protestantism, Roman Catholic and African Independent Churches being prominent; however, there are small communities of Muslims, Hindus, Jews and Pentecostal adherents in South Africa. North Africa and Ethiopia are home to Christianity, Islam and Judaism, as well as being the spiritual homeland of Rastafarianism.

North America

Religion and faith in the United States, Canada and the Caribbean have been influenced by historical migration and colonisation, stressing the importance of religion in public life and community cohesion, and influencing cultural identities and social movements. In Canada and the United States, Christianity predominates, with a wide range of denominations, alongside significant populations of Jews, Muslims, Buddhists and those identifying as unaffiliated or secular, and Indigenous spiritual practices. The Caribbean is marked by a mix of Christianity – particularly Catholicism and Protestantism (including Anglicans, Calvinists, Baptists, Lutherans and Methodists, each with their own distinct theological emphases and practices). African-Caribbean religions such as Vodou are also present, as a result of slavery.

Additionally, in the twentieth and early twenty-first centuries, non-conformist interpretations of Christianity have emerged – for example, individualised or eclectic views of spirituality that are not usually connected to any particular founder; these are often centred on the individual or a group and do not follow established denominational structures or doctrines – often holding the view that there are many different ways to think about God.

South America

Catholicism is the most widely practised Christian denomination, reflecting the region's strong historical ties to the Roman Catholic Church.

Brazil is home to a sizeable population of practitioners and supporters of spiritism, a religious and philosophical doctrine, which has blended into the local way of life and is practised alongside other religious traditions such as Protestantism and Catholicism.

Meanwhile, Orthodox Christianity, though representing a minority tradition in South America, is practised by immigrant communities from Greece, Russia, Syria, Lebanon and Eastern Europe. These Orthodox communities, primarily found in Argentina, Brazil and Chile, have established churches affiliated with various Eastern Orthodox patriarchates, such as the Greek, Russian and Antiochian Orthodox Churches. Despite their minority status, Orthodox Christians in South America maintain their liturgical and spiritual traditions while integrating aspects of local culture. Their churches often serve as cultural centres, preserving the religious and cultural identities of their congregations, alongside cultivating interfaith relations in the region.

Europe

Europe is generally divided into three major branches: Roman Catholicism in the west and southwest; Protestantism in the north; and Eastern Orthodoxy in the east and southeast. Christianity remains a prominent and influential religion, although atheism has a long history. The social secularism trend in nations such as the United Kingdom, Sweden, Denmark and Norway, and the decline in traditional religious affiliation, highlights why the majority of people in these countries identify as agnostic or non-religious.

Oceania

Colonisation aimed at converting Aboriginal people by introducing the Church of England to them spurred missionary efforts. Christianity is said to be the majority religion in Oceania. There are small representations of traditional Indigenous myths and religious practices, which continue to exist. Alongside atheists and agnostics, as well as 'other religions', such as Taoism, Rastafarianism, Scientology and Unitarian Universalism, Buddhism, Islam in Papua, Hinduism in Fiji and Judaism are prominent.

Table 3.1 shows the main religions and belief systems listed in chronological order. A glossary can be found at the end of the book.

Table 3.1 Table of founders, origins, beliefs and customs

Religion/faith	Countries	Founder	Origins	Holy book	Principal beliefs and customs
Hinduism	Bangladesh, India, Indonesia, Mauritius, Nepal, Sri Lanka	No known founder	2000–1500 BCE	Upanishads	Believed to be the oldest religion in the world. It is a polytheistic religion: although there is a belief in one god, good is believed to come in many forms, demonstrated by the various gods and goddesses. There is one primary scripture: the Vedas. The Hindu place of worship is a temple (*Mandir*). Key features include rituals (*yajna*), festivals and pilgrimages. and the philosophical concepts of *dharma* (duty), specifically to family and community life, *karma* (action and reaction), *samsara* (the cycle of rebirth) and *moksha* (liberation from the cycle of rebirth).
Zoroastrianism	India, Iran, North America	Prophet Zoroaster (Zarathustra)	1500–1200 BCE	Avesta	One of the oldest monotheistic religions. The sacred scripture guides followers in theological and ritualistic practices of truthfulness and ethical living towards the triumph of good. Zoroastrianism emphasises the dualism of good (Ahura Mazda), symbolised by fire (purity) and evil (Angra Mainyu).
Taoism/Daoism	China, Hong Kong, Japan, Malaysia, Taiwan	Laozi, the reputed author of the *Tao Te Ching*	Sixth century BCE	Tao Te Ching	Emphasises living in harmony with the Tao (the Way), which represents the fundamental nature of the universe. Key features include the principles of Wu Wei (non-action or effortless action), simplicity, spontaneity and living in harmony with nature. Taoist practices involve meditation, feng shui, martial arts (such as Tai Chi), and rituals aimed at aligning with the Tao. Taoist thought deeply influences Chinese culture, philosophy and medicine.

Table 3.1 (*Cont.*)

Religion/faith	Countries	Founder	Origins	Holy book	Principal beliefs and customs
Jainism	India, Japan	Rishabhanatha	Sixth century BCE	Agamas and the Siddhanta	Stresses non-violence (*ahimsa*) as a cornerstone for achieving an ethical and self-disciplined (ascetic) life, ultimately aiming for the goal of liberation (*moksha*). Crucial to its teachings are the 24 Tirthankaras, along with the concepts of karma and reincarnation.
Buddhism	China, Hong Kong, Japan, Singapore, Sri Lanka, Nepal, Thailand, Taiwan	Siddhartha Gautama (Buddha)	Sixth to fifth century BCE	Tripitaka	Based on Four Noble Truths (suffering and the path to its cessation), and the Eightfold Path (a practical guide to ethical conduct, mental discipline and wisdom). Buddhists practise meditation and mindfulness to achieve liberation and peace of mind (Nirvana). Buddhists believe in reincarnation and karma; it is not about belief in God but rather following a way of life. Shrines to Buddha are found in temples and in the home.
Judaism	United States, Israel	Abraham deemed the patriarch, alongside his son Jacob; Moses regarded as the lawgiver; and David as establishing Jerusalem, the central city. God made covenants with people.	1800 BCE	Torah (first five books of the Old Testament)	One of the world's oldest monotheistic religions. Involves belief in Yahweh as the one and only God. Judaism traces its origins to the 12 tribes of Israel, each representing one of the sons of Jacob. The beliefs and ethical teachings of Judaism adhere to the central scripture. Key religious practices include communal worship and learning in synagogue worship, where prayers and religious rites are conducted, alongside observance of the ten commandments and festivals including Passover, Yom Kippur and Hanukkah, and adherence to dietary (kosher) laws and rituals such as circumcision.

					These symbolise adherence to Jewish identity, acts of kindness and covenant with God. There is a wide range of denominations, from orthodox to liberal, and degrees of adherence to worshipping in a synagogue and maintaining Shabbat (the Sabbath day of rest, from Friday sunset through to Saturday evening).
Catholicism	Brazil, France, Italy, Ireland, Mexico, Philippines, Poland, Spain, United States	St Peter (first Pope)	30 CE	The Bible and Roman Missal	The official establishment of the Catholic Church took centuries, undergoing significant changes in both structure and doctrine. Catholicism can be traced back to Jesus Christ. The apostles in the first century CE, including the first Pope, and several church fathers and saints are important figures. God's nature is the monotheistic belief in the existence of the Trinity – the Father, the Son and the Holy Spirit – in which Jesus Christ is acknowledged as fully human and fully divine.
					The core beliefs emphasise the seven sacraments, the authority of the Pope (the world church's spiritual head), the transubstantiation of the Eucharist (the idea that during the Eucharist, the bread and wine actually become the body and blood of Christ) and saint veneration. Confession, the recitation of the Rosary, pilgrimages and Mass are examples of traditions. The traditions are deeply rooted in liturgical worship, with the Mass, which includes

Table 3.1 (Cont.)

Religion/faith	Countries	Founder	Origins	Holy book	Principal beliefs and customs
					various rituals, prayers and hymns, serving as the central act of communal worship. Other significant customs include the observance of feast days honouring saints and significant occasions in the lives of Christ and the Virgin Mary – viewing them as intercessors who can pray on behalf of the faithful, and the practice of confession. These customs assist Catholics to lead a life that accords with their faith. Baptism, confirmation, reconciliation, anointing of the sick, marriage and Holy Orders are essential means of grace. Catholicism teaches that salvation requires both faith and good works, reflecting a life lived according to Christ's teachings.
Islam	Afghanistan, Bangladesh, India, Indonesia, Iran, Nigeria, Pakistan, Turkey	Prophet Muhammad (considered the final prophet in a line of prophets that includes key figures like Adam, Noah, Abraham, Moses and Jesus [known as Prophet Isa])	622 CE	The Qur'an (Quran)	Islam is a major religion in Asia, founded in the Arabian Peninsula. Islam acknowledges both Judaism and Christianity, viewing them as 'People of the Book'. Muslims believe in Allah as the sole deity (monotheism), all-powerful, merciful and compassionate, who revealed to Muhammad the literal word of God. There are two major sects, Sunni and Shia, differing in certain theological and leadership aspects. The foundations of Muslim/Islamic practices, which are integrated into the daily lives of its followers, include communal worship, the celebration of Eid festivals and dietary laws (halal). Additionally, the Five Pillars of Islam comprise Shahada (declaration of faith), Salah (prayer), Zakat (charity giving), Sawm (fasting during Ramadan) and Hajj (pilgrimage to Mecca).

Sikhism	Canada, India, United Kingdom	Guru Nanak Dev Ji, developed further by ten Sikh Gurus	Fifteenth century	Guru Granth Sahib	The faith focuses upon devotion to one God, Waheguru (Naam Japna); it upholds the principles of equality, integrity, justice and community service. Sikhs believe that all paths ultimately lead to the one true God, granting individuals the freedom to choose their spiritual journey. Key practices include daily remembrance of God's name (*Naam Japna*), earning an honest living (*Kirat Karni*), sharing with others (*Vand Chakna*) and wearing the 'five Ks', including *Kesh* (uncut hair), often covered by a turban. Sikhism also allows for dietary freedom, though many Sikhs choose vegetarianism. Worship takes place in a *Gurdwara*, where the community gathers to pray, serve others and learn from the teachings of the Gurus, while living in accordance with the values of integrity, justice and spiritual devotion.
Protestantism	Denmark, Finland, France, Germany (central, eastern and northern regions), Iceland, Netherlands (central and northern regions), Norway, Sweden, Switzerland, United Kingdom, United States	Martin Luther (German monk and university professor)	1517	The Bible	During the Reformation, a movement that began in 1517 when Martin Luther famously nailed his 95 Theses to the door of the Wittenberg Church. God's nature is characterised by monotheistic belief in the Trinity and a focus on a close, personal relationship with God via Jesus Christ. Luther is credited with founding Lutheranism; other important figures in the Protestant Reformation include John Calvin, whose teachings shaped Calvinism and the Reformed Tradition; and other reformers like Karl Barth, Ulrich Zwingli and John Knox, who contributed to the formation of various Protestant denominations.

→

Table 3.1 (Cont.)

Religion/faith	Countries	Founder	Origins	Holy book	Principal beliefs and customs
					The fundamental doctrine emphasises the priesthood of all believers, sola fide (faith alone), disputing the Catholic beliefs on the papacy and transubstantiation. Other core beliefs are sola scriptura (scripture alone). The Eucharist and baptism are two sacraments recognised by the majority of denominations.
					Protestant worship typically centres on a personal relationship with and faith in God, through Jesus Christ. This is viewed as the foundation of a believer's spiritual life and is cultivated through regular communal worship services, preaching, prayer, Bible reading and study, reflecting its focus on scripture and personal faith. Traditions vary widely among the different denominations but often include congregational singing and the observance of major Christian holidays such as Easter and Christmas.
Quaker, aka Religious Society of Friends	Africa (parts), Australia, Bolivia, Canada, Kenya, North America, United Kingdom	George Fox	1652	N/A	The Quaker movement was founded in England. Fox sought a more direct and personal experience of God, advocating for a form of worship characterised by silence and waiting for divine inspiration, rather than structured rituals and clergy. Central to Quaker beliefs are the principles of equality, simplicity and peace. Quakers emphasise the 'Inner Light', the belief that everyone has access to God's presence within them.

					This focus on personal experience and community-led worship led to a unique religious identity that has influenced social justice movements and practices of non-violence.
Atheism	China, Czech Republic, Denmark, Norway, Sweden	Matthias Knutzen (first known)	1566/ 1571	N/A	Atheism was given a formal definition during the Enlightenment – influenced by ideas of both classical philosophers such as Epicurus and Lucretius and contemporary intellectuals such as Friedrich Nietzsche and Richard Dawkins. Atheism rejects religious or divine beliefs in favour of rational argumentation, factual data and secular theories of the universe's origins. Atheism contends that there is insufficient evidence to prove the existence of gods; hence it refutes the existence of a higher power. Although there are no official rituals or traditions associated with atheism, many atheists share the values of secular humanism or other ethical systems, which emphasise reason and a non-religious way of living.
Spiritism	Argentina, Brazil, France, Portugal, Spain, United States	Allan Kardec (French philosopher)	1857	The Spirits' Book	Spiritism's core doctrines combine aspects of Christianity with ideas about the evolution of spirits and reincarnation, spiritist doctrine and organising their lessons through mediumship, conveyed by spirits. It places a strong emphasis on enhancing morality and ethics via introspection and knowledge of spiritual laws.

Table 3.1 (*Cont.*)

Religion/faith	Countries	Founder	Origins	Holy book	Principal beliefs and customs
Church of Jesus Christ of Latter-Day Saints, aka Mormonism	Brazil, Mexico, United States	Brigham Young, Joseph Smith	1830	Book of Mormon	Mormonist belief is monotheistic, namely that the Godhead is three separate entities: God the Father, Jesus Christ and the Holy Ghost. That exaltation is a possible path for humans to become gods. Brigham Young (leader of the early migrations and successor to Joseph Smith, the founder) are important figures. Mormons believe in continuous revelation, and contemporary prophets are among the core beliefs and traditions, with a focus on missionary work, temple rites and family values.
Adventists of the Seventh Day, aka Adventists or Seventh Day Adventists	Brazil, South Africa, United States	William and Ellen G. White	1863	The Bible	Adventists of the Seventh Day place a strong emphasis on God's monotheistic nature, belief in the Trinity (Father, Son and Holy Spirit) and the imminence of Christ's second coming; they are dedicated to leading a life that is consistent with biblical teachings. White's prophecies and writings stress the importance of keeping Saturday as the Sabbath, health-related ideas like vegetarianism and health and education through hospitals, schools and other establishments.
Witnesses of Jehovah, aka Jehovah's Witnesses	Brazil, Italy, Mexico, Nigeria, United States	Charles Taze Russell (then Joseph Franklin Rutherford)	1931	Emphatic Diaglott or New World Translation of the Holy Scriptures (NWT)	Commonly called 'Witnesses', they believe in a monotheistic God, holding that Jesus Christ is God's son and a separate entity apart from the Trinity, and that Jehovah is the only real God. The faith is renowned for its outreach initiatives and unique practices, including use of the name Jehovah and

					unique practices, including use of the name Jehovah and a belief that God's kingdom will soon be established on Earth. Door-to-door evangelism, refusing to serve in the military and remaining politically neutral are examples of practices.
Agnostic	China, Czech Republic, Denmark, Japan, Sweden	Thomas Huxley	1869	N/A	Agnostics believe gods or the divine exist, but their existence is unknowable. They emphasise scepticism towards religious claims and rely on reason and empirical evidence to navigate the world, contending that it is impossible to know with certainty whether god(s) exist. Agnostics focus on the boundaries of human knowledge rather than endorsing any particular views about the nature of God. Note: Agnosticism is not the same as theism, which affirms belief in gods, or atheism, which denies their existence.
Pentecostalism	Caribbean, Latin America, Oceania, Sub-Saharan Africa, United States	Charles Fox Parham	1873	Holy Book	The early twentieth century saw the emergence of Pentecostalism as a vibrant and significant Christian movement, characterised by significant occurrences like the 1906–09 Azusa street revival in Los Angeles. This revival, which was spearheaded by people like Charles Parham and William J Seymour, was crucial in forming the Pentecostal movement, which spread quickly and continues to expand throughout the United States and other countries. A direct and intimate relationship with God is of paramount

→

Table 3.1 (*Cont.*)

Religion/faith	Countries	Founder	Origins	Holy book	Principal beliefs and customs
					importance in Pentecostalism. The fundamental idea of Pentecostalism is that believers can have a profound and real encounter with the power of the Holy Spirit through baptism. The work and presence of the Holy Spirit are emphasised differently in Pentecostalism than in Protestantism, despite the two movements sharing many fundamental Christian beliefs, such as the authority of scripture and salvation via faith in Jesus Christ. Living a Christian life is not possible without a vibrant, experiential faith life that is marked by spiritual gifts like prophecy, healing and speaking in tongues. Pentecostalism also encompasses other customs such as prayer services, evangelistic outreach and revival meetings, which are designed to reignite believers' faith. A strong emphasis is placed on believers developing a close relationship with God through personal testimony and regular spiritual exercises like Bible reading and prayers.
Rastafarianism	Barbados, Ethiopia, Jamaica, St Lucia	Leonard P. Howell	1935	Jah International Version Holy Bible (King James version)	Rastafarianism took root following Haile Selassie I's coronation as emperor of Ethiopia in 1930 (the primary object of worship), a manifestation of the one true God, Jah, who Rastafarians believe to be the Messiah and the reincarnation of God. They practise monotheism.

					Rooted in a sociopolitical worldview that emphasises a commitment to social justice and a strong sense of identity and purpose for people of African descent, the movement draws heavily from the teachings of Marcus Garvey, a well-known Black nationalist leader who prophesied the return of African descent to Africa, which is viewed as Zion, and rejected Western materialism and cultural domination, which is referred to as 'Babylon'. The movement also emphasises living a natural and spiritual life, which is reflected in their lifestyle choices and religious practices. Wearing dreadlocks as a symbol of the Lion of Judah and a rejection of Babylonian norms, using marijuana (*Ganja*) in religious ceremonies as a sacrament to enhance spiritual experiences and adhering to the Ital diet, which emphasises eating natural, unprocessed foods, are some examples of these practices.
Scientology	Australia, Italy, New Zealand, Portugal, Spain, South Africa, Sweden, United States (especially California)	L. Ron Hubbard	1950s	Dianetics: The ModernScience of Mental Health	The foundational belief is that people are spiritual beings known as Thetans, and that they are enlightened but stuck in physical bodies and need spiritual healing to become free. The healing process is 'auditing', a type of therapy that aims to rid people of painful memories. Scientology places more emphasis on personal spiritual development and self-actualisation than it does on conventional conceptions of God. The Church of Scientology is known for its unusual rituals and practices, such as the use of the E-Meter during auditing sessions.

Table 3.1 (*Cont.*)

| Unitarian Universalism | Central Europe (mostly Romania and Hungary), Ireland, India, Jamaica, Japan, Canada, Nigeria, South Africa, United Kingdom, United States | Representatives such as Hosea Ballou for universalism and William Ellery Channing | 1961 | Many sources of world scriptures: Holy Bible, Koran, Tao De Ching, Torah | Encourages independent, responsible search for meaning and the truth without regard to any one creed. Emphasises respect for different beliefs, social justice and human rights. Due to its inclusive approach to spirituality, religious practices and social issues, it holds that God's nature is non-creedal; therefore, believers can be traditional theists, atheists or agnostics. |

Case study

John, age 36, identifies with a Pentecostal Christian faith, whereas Sara, age 34, identifies as a non-practising Jew. After having successful careers and being financially secure the couple is seeking to adopt a child – they have no desire to have a birth child because they believe there are many children who need a home. They are currently undergoing the adoption assessment process. Among other things, the assessment will need to explore how they plan to navigate potential conflicts and find common ground, ensuring their child is raised in a loving and supportive environment that respects both faith traditions.

Sara was raised in a Jewish household and only participates in her local synagogue, and as such does not strictly observe the Sabbath, although she does during the main religious Jewish holidays. However, due to Judaism being an identity, she adheres to kosher dietary practices. Sara promotes her faith by creating a home environment rich in Jewish culture. She believes in the importance of religious education and wants her child to have a strong sense of identity. John's faith, on the other hand, guides his moral decisions and daily living, including weekly attendance at a Pentecostal church some 10 kilometres from their home – where he is one of the Sunday school teachers, engages in mid-week Bible study and prayer meetings, and believes strongly in the power of prayer, speaking in tongues, and the gifts of the Holy Spirit. John believes in the transformative power of a personal relationship with God through Jesus Christ. John plans to raise his child with a strong Christian foundation, instilling a deep Christian faith in his future child, teaching them the importance of prayer, scripture and the Abrahamic foundations of faith.

Sara plans to incorporate Jewish teachings and values into her parenting. She wants to celebrate Jewish holidays as a family and intends to send the child to a Hebrew school. Sarah is open to her child learning about Christianity. John intends to raise the child with Christian principles, teaching them to pray and read the Bible from a young age. He expects the child to participate in church-related activities. He supports the idea of the child learning about Judaism and celebrating Jewish holidays but feels that Christianity should be the primary influence on the child's spiritual development.

This case presents an opportunity to demonstrate how a couple with different religious beliefs can work together to create a harmonious and faith-filled home for their adopted child.

Reflective exercise

» Using the F.A.I.T.H. Assessment Tool below, complete each section of the tool adding your analysis in the bottom section for reflection.

Faith name	Attitudes and beliefs	Impact	Time commitments	How is faith practised and promoted?
		Including strengths and vulnerabilities (safeguarding)		

Source: Gledhill (2021).

Chapter summary

The chapter's primary focus has been distinguishing between faith humility and cultural humility. For meaningful interaction, knowing the facts about world faiths is not enough. Rather, cultural humility necessitates a compassionate, open-minded attitude that acknowledges the boundaries of one's knowledge and the need for lifelong learning about the experiences of others. This chapter examines the variety of world religions and faiths found on the different continents, highlighting the fundamental ties that every religious tradition has to its own historical, cultural and social setting. Although superficial knowledge alone does not result in true cultural awareness, researching the origins, founders, sacred texts and central rituals of religions provides insightful information about their importance. The chapter encourages the reader to recognise that religion often shapes identity on the personal and social levels. It is imperative to approach individuals from other religious origins with empathy and recognise the profound cultural and spiritual value that faith holds for them in order to interact with them in a respectful manner.

Key takeaways from the chapter

- Religion and faith are central to personal and communal identity, and respectful engagement requires empathy and openness to the unique ways in which people live out their beliefs.

- Engagement and intercultural dialogue are key to understanding and emphasising that respectful communication and genuine curiosity about others' beliefs are more important than factual knowledge alone.

- While religion is often tied to specific countries and regions, migration and globalisation have made faith traditions more complex and widespread, challenging the idea that religions are confined to certain geographic areas.

Chapter 4 | **The 'wounded healer' and the consciousness/constructiveness axle**

Being self-aware is not the absence of mistakes, but the ability to learn and correct them.

Daniel Chidiac (2013)

Introduction

Effective personal and professional judgement (EPPJ) is about accepting the reality that all decision-making is susceptible to the effects of our personal biographies, thus highlighting the importance of using them constructively in our professional role.

An understanding of the concept of the 'wounded healer' can help an individual achieve this. For most people, the notion of the 'wounded healer' conjures up the rather negative view that an individual who has experienced trauma or suffering in their own childhood seeks employment in the caring profession as a means to relieve the suffering of others, but this is not the complete picture. This chapter aims to broaden the reader's understanding of the concept and how it applies to practice in the 'helping' professions.

Definition of the concept

While the wounded healer concept is a powerful metaphor, it is not a psychological theory based on empirical data or validated principles. Instead, it is an archetypal understanding of some individuals who enter the helping and therapeutic process.

The ancient Greek myth

The origins of the wounded healer concept have ancient roots associated with Greek mythology. Ancient philosophy and mythology were intertwined, with philosophers drawing on mythological stories to illustrate moral, ethical or educational principles. One prominent figure in Greek mythology is Kheiron (spelt Chiron in Latin), who lived from the fifth to the fourth century BCE, associated with the classical period of Greek civilisation. He was said to be a centaur, a creature with the upper body of a human and the lower body of a horse. His parents were Titan Cronus (Saturn) and the sea nymph Philyra. The latter is said to have rejected Kheiron due to being horrified by her son's appearance. Kheiron prayed to the gods, and the gods granted his request to be different from the other centaurs; his body was transformed into a unique hybrid, in that he retained the upper body of a human, including his intellect, facial features and arms. But alongside the customary horse's body and legs, his lower half remained human, with legs extending from his torso. Additionally, unlike his counterparts, he is described as being of noble character, gentle, wise, intelligent and skilled in many areas, including being renowned for his skills in medicine, as the greatest physician of the time.

Kheiron is said to have been accidentally wounded during a battle when a poisoned arrow, aimed at another, struck him. Despite possessing the ability, knowledge and skill to heal others, Kheiron was unable to heal himself. Being immortal, he was left in immense pain, unable to find a remedy for his own suffering. Eventually, seeking relief from his physical and mental agony, Kheiron asked the gods to exchange his immortality with that of Prometheus, who was being subjected to daily physical and mental torture for defying the gods. Kheiron's request was granted, and he gave up his immortality, allowing Prometheus to be freed.

Kheiron's life illustrates the paradox of being a healer who carries their own wounds unhealed. Thus, the myth of Kheiron serves as a foundational narrative for the birth of the wounded healer archetype and understanding it. It resonated across cultures and disciplines, a symbolic narrative of the complexities and paradoxes inherent in the healing process. The wounded healer archetype that Kheiron represents is highlighted in these features of his life:

» childhood and adult trauma – rejected by his mother at birth and accidentally poisoned;

» suffering the effects of past hurts;

» the ability to use personal suffering to help/teach others;

» sacrifice and transformation – giving of self so others do not experience the same suffering and pain.

Jung

The myth of Kheiron, initially orally transmitted and then later recorded in written form, has had an enduring nature, influencing philosophy and psychology in more recent times through Carl Jung. Jung, a psychiatrist and psychoanalyst, delved into the wounded healer archetype, drawing inspiration from mythological figures such as Kheiron. Jung explored the idea of wounded healers in the broader context of archetypes and the collective unconscious. He gave the above interpretation a new slant in 1961 when he expressed the view that those entering the helping professions unsurprisingly brought their biographic experiences to their professional performance. The wounded healer archetype, as conceptualised by Jung, refers to individuals who have undergone profound suffering or personal struggles and, as a result, gain the capacity to heal and guide others. By incorporating the archetype into his theories of analytical psychology, Jung theorised that these adverse experiences provided unique insights for the wounded healer, which could be used empathically in the performance of their role. As Jung put it:

> *For only what [the doctor] can put right in himself can he hope to put right in the patient... This, and nothing else, is the meaning of the Greek myth of the wounded physician.*
>
> (1993, p 21)

This, however, would require the wounded healer to be aware of, and manage, their conscious and unconscious personality. Jung emphasised the transformative potential of embracing one's wounds and using them as a source of healing for others.

In summary, Jung originally initiated the use of the concept in the field of psychology to refer to individuals who, despite having experienced personal struggles, trauma or psychological wounds, use those very challenges to empathise with and help others in their healing journeys. It suggests that the healer's own experiences of suffering and overcoming difficulties contribute to their ability to understand and support others who are going through similar struggles.

Modern thinkers

The link between Kheiron and the wounded healer archetype has become more explicit in psychological and mythological discussions in the twentieth and twenty-first centuries. Contemporary authors and scholars, particularly those in the fields of mythology and psychology, have explored the symbolic significance of Kheiron in relation to mentorship, teaching and the wide-ranging nature of healing. Bolen (1989), a psychiatrist and Jungian psychologist, explored Kheiron's symbolism as a mentor and healer, and the implications of his myth in contemporary cultural and psychological contexts. Specifically, she examined the significance of Kheiron, the archetypal wounded healer, for personal growth and healing.

The relevance of the wounded healer in social work

The concept and the consciousness/constructiveness axle

The doctoral social work research from Weekes (2020) that birthed the idea for this book notes the oxymoron in the concept of the wounded healer, at times invoking a negative view about individuals who, having experienced personal suffering and trauma, seek employment in the caring profession, motivated by a desire to relieve the suffering of others. Jung (1961) added to Freud's theory of countertransference by suggesting that those entering the helping professions unsurprisingly brought their biographic experiences to their professional performance, providing unique insights for the wounded healer that could be used empathically in the performance of their role. However, this required the wounded healer to be aware of and manage their conscious and unconscious personality characteristics. Such ideas about the emotional self-awareness of individuals can be aligned to the function within organisations, addressing questions about whether personal biographies can be used constructively and effectively in decision-making. The study showed that some individuals were sufficiently aware of themselves to make effective contributions, while others demonstrated lower levels of self-awareness and were largely unaware of themselves, which meant their contributions were less effective. Still others, although not totally aware, could perhaps be supported and trained to make a more effective use of self in performing their task.

A visual representation of the impact of biography, mathematically plotted on the linear scatter diagram, illustrates whether bringing the self to the task/role is effective (Figure 4.1).

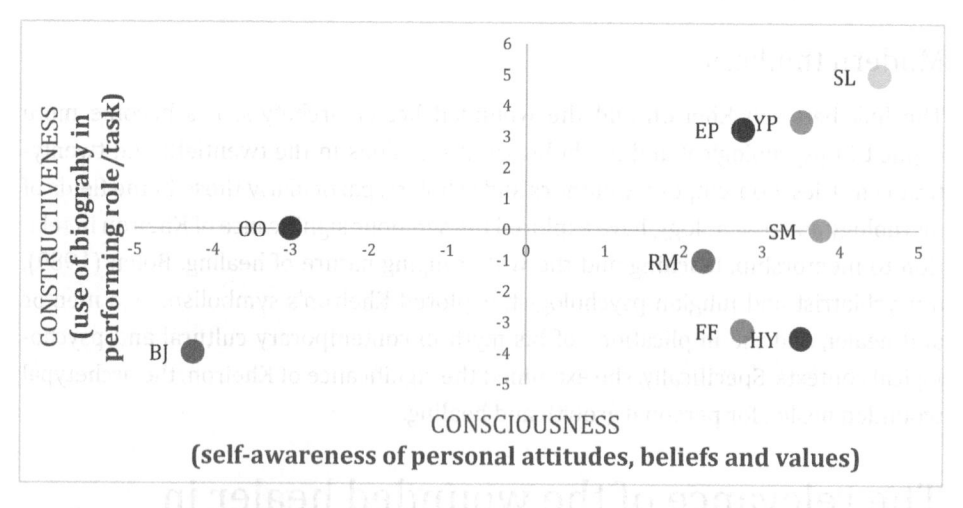

Figure 4.1 'Wounded healer' axle

The three interviewees in the top-right box articulate how they have processed their conscious, personal material in their thinking and recommendation-making. Their narrative gave a clear sense of who they were as individuals and, while on the panel, they were observed to be able to bring this awareness to their role. The four interviewees in the bottom right box would commonly be described as professionals and good practitioners who are able to get the job done. They would appear not to be easily riled and do not bring personal issues to work. In their narratives, three shared little about themselves, appearing at times distant and detached. While this may appear to be an admirable quality in practice, such individuals may not come across as personable and understanding of the plight of others. Two interviewees sit in the bottom left box, both able to talk about the sum of their life experiences in their narratives. The final quadrant is, perhaps unsurprisingly, empty. The study shows that a panel member is unlikely to be both highly conscious and ineffective. Although it is acknowledged that it is possible that an individual may be having a bad day or is being particularly triggered by certain material, aware individuals will not usually be located here.

The wounded healer in social work training and practice

In the field of social work, this concept is particularly relevant, manifesting itself in various ways. Social workers often encounter individuals and communities who are facing complex and challenging issues. The social workers' own personal experiences of challenges, struggles and trauma can contribute to their ability to be effective and empathic while undertaking their role in the profession. The concept is being used more in social work research. Gilbert and Stickley (2012) expressed that if a quarter of the population experiences mental health difficulties and if one in four of the population is affected by mental health problems, inevitably social work professionals in mental healthcare settings must also be experiencing them. Newcomb et al's (2015) article reviews how teaching institutions can provide students with the knowledge to use their childhood experiences of adversity positively to heal others. Straussner et al's (2018) study, which explores the age, gender, ethnicity, race and mental health of their social work participants, identifies that a large proportion of participants could be classified as 'wounded healers'. Mackay (2023), sharing her personal experiences, recognised the dichotomy of fearing and hiding her lived experiences while being encouraged to champion the expertise of service-users in the design of services. She suggests that, as a wounded healer, it is important to utilise personal lived experiences while understanding the power dynamics and clear boundary lines of being a professional when working with service-users.

Implications of the wounded healer

In terms of application, the concept of the wounded healer has implications for the fostering of relationships between service-users and social workers, and between social workers and colleagues in their organisations, but also in inter-agency and multi-agency settings. Some of the negative and positive aspects are highlighted below.

Negative impact of the wounded healer

If experiences resonate with the social worker, there could be a risk of over-identifying with service-users because of empathising with them due to having the same or similar personal experiences. Having a heightened emotional reaction, possibly based on one's own unresolved issues, can equally lead to countertransference, a loss of objectivity potentially resulting in a degree of role confusion. There is a risk of burnout if the wounded healer struggles with their professional responsibilities and maintaining their own well-being, leading to exhaustion and ultimately ineffectiveness. The five 'Cs' to be mindful of are as follows.

1. *Countertransference.* This refers to the social worker's personal triggers, needs and conflicts, which surface at both a conscious and unconscious level, in response to the emotional and behavioural aspects that the service-user brings. When working with the service-user, the social worker is unconsciously triggered by their unresolved issues, only viewing the service-user's situation through the lens of their own experiences. This countertransference affects the objectivity of the social worker, hindering the working relationship, as the social worker may unconsciously project their own unresolved issues onto the service-user.

2. *Crisis trigger.* The social worker's unresolved issues may be intensified or could resurface due to the service-user's ongoing presenting challenges. The unaddressed issues may pull the social worker into crisis, impacting their ability to effectively focus and support the service-user.

3. *Codependence.* When the social worker's self-worth is overly linked to the success or progress of the service-user, the social worker may feel that pressure to appear 'healed' could create internal conflict. Alternatively, the social worker may unintentionally impose their own expectations or values on the service-user if the responses to interventions or paths to resolving issues mirror their own experiences, thus placing unrealistic expectations on the service-user's progress. The social worker will inevitably lead to their disappointment or frustration. As the service-user is not them, we are all unique and need a person-centred approach to our issues. Conversely, the service-users may in turn put unrealistic expectations on the social worker to be 'perfect' and have overcome their own challenges. Thus, there is a risk that the relationship between the service-user and social worker can be overly affected, leading to a loss of independence and growth on the part of the service-user, as both parties struggle with their codependence.

4. *Compassion fatigue.* The heightened emotional and personal investment from and toll on the social worker of supporting the service-user can lead to burnout, exhaustion and decreased effectiveness in the task and role as the social worker unconsciously vicariously attempts to manage their own trauma and well-being alongside meeting the real and perceived needs of the service-user.

5. *Confusion of roles.* The social worker may struggle ethically to maintain clear professional boundaries, albeit consciously aware of the distinction between their personal experiences and the needs of the service-user, thus blurring boundaries. As they manage the challenges of being empathetic versus inappropriate disclosures or over-involvement, alongside objectivity versus compromising their passion for helping, objective decision-making can be put at risk due to over-identifying as a result of being too emotionally invested or personally affected. This can compromise ethical standards and professional boundaries.

Professionals need to be conscious of the negative aspects of the archetype, so must:

» engage in continual self-reflection, to ensure the maintenance of professional boundaries;

» seek supervision, to address personal issues through appropriate channels;

» prioritise their own well-being to manage their mental health.

The positive impact of the wounded healer

Those who have experienced personal adversity or trauma can be well placed to help others if they understand their own vulnerabilities and wounds in a way that enables them to offer compassionate and responsive support to service-users. By using self-reflection to maintain healthy professional boundaries, social workers who are attuned to and self-aware of their own vulnerabilities can connect with service-users. Below are five 'Es' to promote the benefits of being conscious of the self brought to the role.

1. *Empathic.* Social workers who have overcome challenges can bring empathy to their working relationships, often due to an inherent understanding of the service-user's struggles. This heightened sensitivity enables them to respond to and adapt interventions to meet the service-user's unique circumstances. This connection, based upon a nuanced cultural insight of common experiences, can create and enhance the rapport and trust in the relationship.

2. *Empowering*. The connection brought about by having and sharing an understanding of experience and trauma can lead to service-users feeling that barriers between themselves and the worker, and to some extent the agency, are less threatening. Service-users might expect a wounded healer to be more authentic and open, making them feel less isolated and more empowered, inspired and motivated because of viewing the stigma of being a service-user through the eyes of a social worker. The social worker who appears to be more compassionate due to knowing what the experience is like can demonstrate that healing is possible, even in the face of adversity.

3. *Enrichment*. The wounded healer, in the role of the social worker, shares personal insight and understanding to the relationship, demonstrating through their personal journey a form of role-modelling that shows overcoming adversity is possible. This can strengthen the service-user's belief in their own coping abilities, recovery and resilience.

4. *Engaging*. Having had personal experience, the social worker can often be more relatable and connectable, which fosters a greater level of engagement between them (and the service) and the service-user by validating the latter's situation. This involves actively guiding, encouraging and supporting service-users in the process of overcoming adversity and effective change through collaborative and shared responsibility in the working relationship and subsequent interventions.

5. *Equitability*. The social worker who is a wounded healer understands that the uniqueness of their own cultural personal experiences contributes to increased cultural humility. By recognising the importance of having to navigate the complexities of diverse backgrounds and experiences, they can be a catalyst for change by demonstrating to other professionals and service-users that transformation is possible.

Addressing the issue of the wounded healer

To address potential issues related to being a wounded healer, social workers need to continually engage in self-reflection to heighten their awareness of personal biases so as not to adversely impact on their relationships with service-users and colleagues. This means being client- and person-centred, collaborative and empowering, reviewing assumptions and not adhering to rigid preconceived expectations and notions. Equally, it means having a flexible, collaborative approach and cultivating a culture of cultural humility.

How can supervisors support social workers with issues from their past?

Supervisors are crucial for supporting social workers, whether they are wounded healers or not. However, if social workers do have personal wounds or struggles, Morrison and Wonnacott's (2010) 4 × 4 × 4 model (Figure 4.2) is one tool that can be used, as supervisors must identify this is the case for the safety of all concerned, to mitigate against any countertransference. They must ensure regular formal and informal supervision and encourage the social worker to engage in self-reflection to explore how they draw on personal insight while finding ways to maintain objectivity, emphasise, role-model and promote the importance of self-care. Specifying and guiding the social worker towards the maintenance of ethical and professional boundaries can further be supported through peer support and further training.

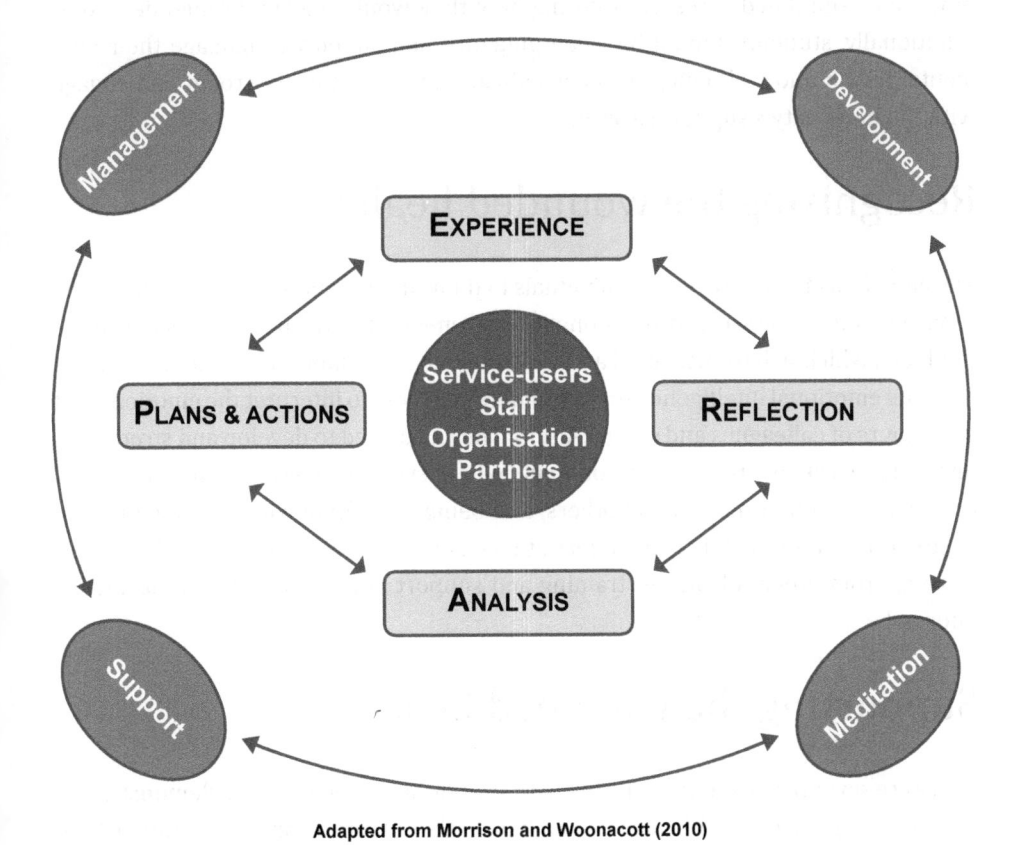

Adapted from Morrison and Woonacott (2010)

Figure 4.2 4x4x4 model

How can university lecturers support student social workers with issues from their past?

Lecturers can issue the pedagogical approaches adopted and contribute to the holistic development of the student to assist them in navigating their personal and professional growth beyond merely attaining academic success. Formative and summative assignments should encourage critical reflection tasks to encourage students to reflect on how their personal experiences may intersect with their emerging professional identity. Lectures and seminars should use case-based learning: simulation, guest speakers and role-play should be used to foster experiential, collaborative group work, cultivating safe spaces for students to share their thoughts and experiences related to the wounded healer concept. Class debates and ethical dilemma discussions are also forums, alongside practice/field placements, where students can reflect on direct practice or simulated cases, considering how they would make informed decisions. Additionally, students should be given guidance and support to manage their own mental health and well-being through self-care advice in the classroom and engage with the university's support services.

Recognising the wounded healer

The aim of this book is to assist individuals in their understanding that increased personal awareness increases professional effectiveness. One way to do this is to use the EPPJ tool, which will be discussed and explained in later chapters. Individuals need to cultivate emotional intelligence so they understand how to interpret the emotions and behaviours of colleagues and service-users. They also need to develop and strengthen interpersonal skills, creating environments where everyone feels safe and supported. Critical reflection of the self and others, and being mindful of what is being brought to situations and how this may impact others, is also valuable. Be genuinely open to learning from other colleagues, training and support networks – whether formal or informal.

Supporting the wounded healer

There are several steps that can be taken to support a colleague who is demonstrating signs of being a wounded healer, remembering that this is an archetype rather than a clinical diagnosis. Initiate a private and confidential, non-confrontational, supportive conversation – where you share your concerns and desire to offer assistance and support. During the conversation, engage in empathetic, active listening, which will provide a safe and validating space for the colleague to share any feelings and challenges. Be guided by your colleague in terms of next steps – whether that is to engage with well-being activities, support services, managers or regular follow-up checks with them – in the development of strategies to manage the challenges brought to bear from being a wounded healer.

All wounded healers need support with conscious and unconscious self-disclosure, ensuring that experiences are shared and used infrequently, and only where relevant and for the benefit of the service-user (Sherlock, 1953). The research on which EPPJ is based showed that people varied in their self-awareness and their ability to use this to make an effective contribution to decision-making. In fact, four distinct categories of consciousness/constructiveness were identified by Weekes (2021).

1. *High consciousness and high constructiveness.* These are individuals who have an awareness both of the self and external factors – which results in more constructive decision-making.

2. *Low consciousness and high constructiveness.* This characterises a less self-aware individual who appears competent in their decision-making, but comes across as mechanical and detached.

3. *Low consciousness and low constructiveness.* These individuals are generally unaware of their internal influences, so are not constructive in decision-making.

4. *High consciousness and low constructiveness.* This characterises a self-aware individual who chooses not to use their awareness constructively in decision-making.

Personal biography at work: some real-life examples

The following are examples of how bias resulting from a person's background can affect their behaviour.

Example 1: low consciousness and low constructiveness

Lucy is a white British female with a stable and supportive family background. In her final year as a social work student, she worked with a white female aged 15 years who had suicidal thoughts and low self-esteem. Lucy discovered that the young female had an eating disorder that she hid from others, as she did not want to be seen as strange. Lucy found this hard to understand, as her happy childhood and supportive family background meant she had lots of friends, loved life and had a great relationship with food.

Example 2: high consciousness and high constructiveness

When a social worker learned that some young people had no money on their school lunch cards, as their parents could not afford it, she ensured that every young person known to her team could get a lunch ticket from her department if they wanted one. Several of the school's staff did not agree with this solution, and publicly questioned young people regarding the legitimacy of their lunch request. This affected their self-esteem. As a result, the social worker decided to give up her own lunch to ensure young people did not face this questioning. When asked why she was willing to do this, she replied that while at school she had free school meals, and had once been humiliated by a dinner lady for using a friend's paid-for ticket. The social worker therefore understood how the young people on free school meals felt.

Example 3: high consciousness and low constructiveness

During her placement, a Black British social work student was discussing aspects of anti-oppressive and anti-discriminatory practice with her supervisor. The student was asked about the racial and cultural make-up of the service-user group with which she was working. The student replied that it was white British. When the supervisor replied that this was surprising, as the area was a diverse community, the student related how she had observed a Black Caribbean and an Asian person access the service on one occasion, but they did not return. When asked why she thought this was the case, the student reflected on her feelings on being in placement as the only Black staff member and how institutional racism is subtle: while organisations claim their services are for everyone, they never mention how everyone using the service comes from one racial or cultural group.

> ### Reflective exercise
>
> Think about a challenging experience or hardship you have faced in your life. What was it, and how did it impact you?
>
> » Consider how this experience has shaped your understanding of empathy and compassion.
>
> » What strengths or coping mechanisms were developed to overcome this challenge.

» Self-assess your comfort level in relation to the following statements.

Statement	Strongly disagree 1	Disagree 2	Neither agree nor disagree 3	Agree 4	Strongly agree 5
I am comfortable acknowledging my own vulnerabilities.					
I find that I can empathise with others who are going through difficult times.					
I often feel a sense of fulfilment when helping others navigate their challenges.					
I am open to recognising the potential growth and learning in my own life experiences.					

» Write a paragraph synthesising your reflections and self-assessment results.
» Consider whether you express traits of being a wounded healer and, if so, in what ways.
» Ponder on how the insights gained from the chapter and activity may influence future roles or career paths.

Case study

Recognising the 'wounded healer' in others

Grace is a children's senior social worker, with 15 years' experience. She is highly regarded for her dedication and commitment in advocating for the rights of children and families. Recently, Grace has been assigned a challenging case involving a family with a history of substance abuse, domestic violence and child neglect.

You have observed that Grace is working excessive hours since being allocated the case – and when other social workers discuss the case relating to the father, she becomes very angry. The case appears to be triggering strong emotions and memories from Grace's own childhood, as she grew up in a household with similar challenges.

At a team training event two years ago, Grace shared that, as a child, she witnessed repeated violent confrontations between her parents. Her father struggled with alcohol addiction and her mother's anger issues. The sound of raised voices, breaking objects and physical violence became a routine part of her daily life. Her parents' personal difficulties meant they struggled to provide consistent care, neglecting her needs and those of her siblings, such as proper meals, hygiene and supervision. The eldest sibling, Grace, assumed a caretaker role for her brothers and sisters, which impacted her own childhood and development. Alongside her home life, she was bullied at school due to children in her small town being aware of her home circumstances, which affected Grace's academic performance. As a teenager, she was involved in extracurricular programmes due to being encouraged by teachers and mentors who provided her with support so she was able to realise her potential.

Reflective exercise

» How might you support Grace and who might you talk to about what you are observing?

Chapter summary

This chapter has sought to assist the reader to grapple with the idea that no one comes to the role of the social worker as a blank sheet. We all have experiences that impact our lives for good or ill. The chapter has sought to examine how those with lived experience function in their role, exploring the commonly held idea of the wounded healer while perhaps not understanding the Kheiron origins of the myth. Many social workers and mental health professionals have explored and written about the concept of the wounded healer, drawing on various perspectives and experiences.

The concept underscores the idea that healing is often a reciprocal process, where the healer's own experiences of pain and growth contribute significantly to their effectiveness in helping others.

Our increased recognition of the value of understanding and providing services with a real knowledge of the experiences of those with lived experiences underscores the advantages of employing staff who have experienced trauma. Nonetheless, it would be remiss not to acknowledge the inherent potential for complications. Thus, to ensure the safety issues for all concerned, an understanding is needed by individuals, as identified by Sherlock (1953, p 61):

> *The worker must be able to have self-knowledge to the degree of knowing and controlling factors in [their] own personality and motivation that are likely to cause [them] to judge the client.*

As well as employers being aware of the potential risks and benefits of early childhood adversity and adult life experiences, individuals are likely to need support with their sometimes conscious and often unconscious self-disclosure and projections because of their lived experiences to ensure the benefits of them being wounded healers are not overshadowed by the drawbacks to service-users.

The central finding of the research is that to be more conscious of what individuals bring to their respective roles, they will be able to be more constructive in performing the task of recommendation-making. The illuminating finding was the extent to which biography – personal values, beliefs and thinking – significantly pervades decision-making and thus impacts personal and organisational effectiveness. Although highlighted increasingly in other professional areas, it is still under-researched and thus inadequately understood in social work practice. A naive presumption exists that the teaching of anti-oppressive practice and reflection to trainee social workers will automatically result in more self-controlled and self-aware practitioners. Ongoing training and opportunities are required to explore what we all bring to the role.

Social workers who adopt and truly understand the wounded healer concept should have no personal expectations of service-users, recognising that they have the self-efficacy to be experts in their own lives, free to make their own informed choices based on their individual life goals. Thus, to work with service-users to foster their independence in an empowering manner requires a collaborative, client-centred partnership approach to the 'helping' relationship, minimising the usual power imbalance form of practice. Crucial to this approach is effective communication, ongoing self-reflection and transparency, and the maintenance of professional boundaries on the part of the social worker wounded healer rather than a professional arrogance that presupposes they have no issues or that all the social worker's issues have been resolved – as if this were even possible!

Key takeaways from the chapter

- While the wounded healer concept can be a valuable framework in social work, it is important for professionals to strike a balance between using personal experiences to enhance their practice and maintaining the necessary professional boundaries to ensure ethical and effective service delivery.

- This wounded healer archetype emphasises the transformative power of personal challenges in developing empathy, insight and a deeper understanding of human suffering. The idea is that individuals who have faced and addressed their own psychological wounds may be better equipped to guide and assist others on their paths to healing.

- Research shows that people vary in their self-awareness and their ability to use this self-awareness in their decision-making.

- In this regard, EPPJ identifies four categories:
  - high consciousness and high constructiveness;
  - low consciousness and high constructiveness;
  - low consciousness and low constructiveness;
  - high consciousness and low constructiveness.

Chapter 5 | Factors affecting decision-making processes

Truly successful decision-making relies on a balance between deliberate and instinctive thinking.

Malcom Gladwell (2005)

Introduction

Decision-making is a fundamental cognitive process that involves selecting a course of action from multiple alternatives. The complexity of decision-making arises from the multitude of factors that can influence the process. These factors can be broadly categorised into individual, social and environmental influences. Understanding these factors is crucial for improving decision-making strategies in various contexts, from personal choices to organisational decisions. This chapter explores the key factors affecting decision-making processes, supported by the relevant academic literature.

Individual factors

Individual factors pertain to the characteristics intrinsic to the person making the decision. These include cognitive abilities, emotional states, personality traits and biases.

Cognitive abilities

Cognitive abilities such as intelligence, memory and attention significantly impact decision-making. High cognitive ability is associated with better information processing and problem-solving skills, leading to more rational decisions (Stanovich and West, 2000). Conversely, cognitive limitations can result in simplified decision strategies, such as relying on heuristics (Gigerenzer and Gaissmaier, 2011).

Emotional states

Emotions play a crucial role in decision-making. Positive emotions can enhance creativity and the willingness to take risks (Isen, 2001), while negative emotions, such as fear and anxiety, may lead to risk-averse behaviour (Lerner and Keltner, 2001).

The somatic marker hypothesis suggests that emotions serve as markers that guide decision-making, especially under conditions of uncertainty (Damasio, 1994).

Personality traits

Personality traits, as described by the Five-Factor Model (Costa and McCrae, 1992), influence decision-making styles. For instance, individuals high in conscientiousness tend to be thorough and cautious, leading to more deliberate decisions (Roberts et al, 2009). In contrast, those high in extraversion may favour more spontaneous and risky decisions (Judge and Ilies, 2002).

Biases and heuristics

Cognitive biases and heuristics, while often leading to suboptimal decisions, are an integral part of human decision-making. Common biases include confirmation bias, where individuals favour information that confirms their preconceptions (Nickerson, 1998), and over-confidence bias, where individuals overestimate their knowledge or abilities (Moore and Healy, 2008). Heuristics, such as the availability heuristic, involve making decisions based on easily retrievable information (Tversky and Kahneman, 1974).

Social factors

Social factors encompass the influence of other people on an individual's decision-making process. These include social norms, group dynamics and cultural influences.

Social norms

Social norms are the accepted behaviours within a society or group. They can significantly shape decision-making by providing a framework for what is considered appropriate or acceptable. Conformity to social norms is often driven by a desire for social acceptance and a fear of social sanctions (Cialdini and Goldstein, 2004).

Group dynamics

Group dynamics play a critical role in decision-making within teams and organisations. Groupthink, a phenomenon whereby the desire for harmony or conformity results in irrational or dysfunctional decision-making, can lead to poor outcomes (Janis, 1972). However, diversity in groups can enhance decision-making by bringing multiple perspectives and reducing the likelihood of groupthink (Nemeth, 1986).

Cultural influences

Cultural values and practices profoundly influence decision-making processes. Hofstede's (1980) cultural dimensions theory highlights how different cultural contexts, such as individualism versus collectivism, can affect decision preferences. For instance, collectivist cultures may prioritise group harmony and consensus while individualist cultures may value autonomy and individual choice (Triandis, 1995).

Environmental factors

Environmental factors refer to external conditions and stimuli that impact decision-making. These include situational context, economic conditions and technological advancements.

Situational context

The situational context, including the specific circumstances and pressures surrounding a decision, can influence the decision-making process. For example, time pressure often forces individuals to rely on heuristics rather than thorough analysis (Payne et al, 1993). Similarly, high-stakes environments such as medical or military settings may necessitate quick and decisive action, sometimes at the expense of comprehensive deliberation (Klein, 2008).

Economic conditions

Economic conditions, both at the macro and micro levels, impact decision-making. Economic stability and prosperity can lead to more risk-taking behaviours, while economic uncertainty or downturns often result in more conservative and risk-averse decisions (Mian and Sufi, 2014). Additionally, personal financial status can affect individual decisions, such as career choices or investment strategies (Thaler, 1999).

Technological advancements

Technological advancements have transformed the decision-making landscape. Access to vast amounts of information through the internet and big data analytics allows for more informed decisions (Brynjolfsson and McAfee, 2014). However, the complexity and volume of information can also lead to information overload, complicating the decision-making process (Bawden and Robinson, 2009).

Psychological theories and models

Several psychological theories and models provide frameworks for understanding decision-making processes. These include rational choice theory, bounded rationality and dual-process theories.

Rational choice theory

Rational choice theory posits that individuals make decisions by weighing the costs and benefits of different options to maximise utility (Becker, 1976). This model assumes that individuals have access to complete information and can process this information rationally. However, real-world decision-making often deviates from this ideal due to limitations in information and cognitive processing.

Bounded rationality

Herbert Simon's (1957) concept of bounded rationality challenges the assumptions of rational choice theory. Bounded rationality suggests that individuals are limited by their cognitive capabilities and the information available to them. As a result, they use satisficing – a process of choosing an option that meets a satisfactory level rather than the optimal one.

Dual-process theories

Dual-process theories propose that decision-making involves two distinct cognitive systems: System 1, which is fast, automatic and intuitive; and System 2, which is slow, deliberate and analytical (Kahneman, 2011). System 1 is useful for quick decisions in familiar situations, but it can be prone to biases. System 2, while more accurate, is resource-intensive and slower, often reserved for complex and novel decisions.

Neurobiological perspectives

Advances in neuroscience have provided insights into the brain mechanisms underlying decision-making. Key brain regions involved in decision-making include the prefrontal cortex, amygdala and striatum.

Prefrontal cortex

The prefrontal cortex (PFC) is critical for higher-order cognitive functions, including planning, reasoning and decision-making. It is involved in evaluating options, considering future consequences and exerting self-control (Miller and Cohen, 2001). Damage to the PFC can result in impaired decision-making, which is often characterised by impulsivity and poor judgement (Bechara et al, 2000).

Amygdala

The amygdala plays a central role in processing emotions and is particularly important in decisions involving risk and reward (LeDoux, 2000). It helps to assess the emotional significance of stimuli and can influence decision-making by generating emotional responses that inform choices (Phelps, 2006).

Striatum

The striatum is involved in reward processing and habit formation. It integrates information about potential rewards and helps guide decisions based on past experiences of reward and punishment (Montague et al, 2006). Dysfunction in the striatum can lead to disorders of decision-making, such as addiction (Redish et al, 2008).

Organisational decision-making

In organisational contexts, decision-making involves additional layers of complexity due to hierarchical structures, organisational culture and stakeholder interests.

Hierarchical structures

Hierarchical structures in organisations can impact decision-making processes by centralising or decentralising authority. Centralised decision-making often leads to more consistent and controlled decisions, but it can stifle innovation and responsiveness (Mintzberg, 1979). Decentralised decision-making promotes autonomy and flexibility but can result in inconsistencies and coordination challenges (Mintzberg, 1980).

Organisational culture

Organisational culture, defined by shared values, beliefs and practices, shapes decision-making behaviours within an organisation. A culture that promotes openness and learning encourages innovative decision-making, while a risk-averse culture may hinder it (Schein, 1992). Leaders play a critical role in shaping and sustaining organisational culture, thereby influencing decision-making processes (Deal and Kennedy, 1982).

Stakeholder interests

Organisational decisions often involve balancing the interests of various stakeholders, including employees, customers, shareholders and the community. Effective decision-making requires considering the potential impact on all stakeholders and striving for decisions that align with the organisation's mission and values (Freeman, 1984).

Ethical considerations

Ethics play a crucial role in decision-making, particularly in situations involving moral dilemmas or conflicts of interest. Ethical decision-making requires adherence to principles such as fairness, honesty and respect for others.

Moral frameworks

Moral frameworks, such as utilitarianism and deontological ethics, provide guidelines for ethical decision-making. Utilitarianism advocates for decisions that maximise overall happiness and minimise harm (Mill, 1861). Deontological ethics, on the other hand, emphasises adherence to moral rules and duties, regardless of the outcomes (Kant, 1785).

Corporate social responsibility

In organisational contexts, corporate social responsibility (CSR) reflects the ethical obligation of businesses to contribute positively to society. CSR initiatives can influence decision-making by integrating social and environmental considerations into business strategies (Carroll, 1991). Companies with strong CSR commitments often make decisions that go beyond profit maximisation to include social and environmental stewardship.

Ethical leadership

Ethical leadership is crucial for fostering an ethical climate within organisations. Ethical leaders model ethical behaviour, establish clear ethical standards and create an environment where ethical decision-making is valued and supported (Brown and Treviño, 2006). This can enhance trust and cooperation among employees and stakeholders, leading to more sustainable and ethical organisational outcomes.

Enhancing decision-making skills

Improving decision-making skills involves developing cognitive and emotional competencies, leveraging technology and fostering a supportive environment.

Cognitive and emotional competencies

Training in critical thinking and emotional intelligence can enhance decision-making abilities. Critical thinking involves analysing and evaluating information systematically to make reasoned judgements (Facione, 1990). Emotional intelligence, which includes skills such as self-awareness and empathy, helps individuals manage emotions and understand others' perspectives, leading to better interpersonal decisions (Goleman, 1995).

Leveraging technology

Technology, including decision support systems and artificial intelligence, can augment human decision-making by providing data-driven insights and reducing cognitive load (Turban et al, 2011). These tools can assist in analysing complex data, identifying patterns and suggesting optimal courses of action.

Fostering a supportive environment

Creating an environment that supports effective decision-making involves promoting open communication, encouraging diverse perspectives and providing adequate resources and time for decision-making processes. Organisational policies and practices should facilitate collaboration, continuous learning and risk-taking within a framework of accountability.

Case study

Taiwo

Taiwo is a 60 year-old woman of dual heritage – her mother was born in the Caribbean, coming to the United Kingdom in the 1960s, and her father came from West Africa in the late 1970s. Taiwo has a physical disability and works as an administrative assistant in a corporate firm. She faces multiple forms of discrimination due to her disability, age, gender and socioeconomic status.

Reflective exercise

Capture personal reflections and individual thoughts

» Using the table below, critically reflect on how your personal values/beliefs support or hinder your decision-making in the above case study using the three main headings. Choose a model of reflections when completing this task. Examples are provided in the table to help you get started.

Individual factors	Social factors	Environmental factors
eg Having personal values such as a strong work ethic impacts my decision-making.	eg Growing up outside the UK impacts my decision-making.	eg I rely on data and systems to generate decision for me.

Chapter summary

Decision-making is a multifaceted process influenced by a variety of individual, social and environmental factors. Understanding these factors can help individuals and organisations to make more informed and effective decisions. By integrating insights from psychology, neuroscience and organisational behaviour, decision-makers can develop strategies to enhance their decision-making skills and outcomes. Ethical considerations and the role of technology further underscore the complexity and significance of decision-making in contemporary contexts.

Key takeaways from this chapter

- A number of factors affect decision-making, including individual, environmental and social factors.
- Decision-making can take place individually, collectively and organisationally.
- Ethics must always be considered in decision-making.

Chapter 6 | Group decision-making processes

If we create a framework for decision-making that is biased toward life, supportive of families, and fair to people of all circumstances, our policies, legislation, and commercial decisions will be vastly different.

Blase J Cupich (2015)

Introduction

This chapter introduces you to key concepts and thinking about group decision-making. It explores whether group decision-making is more effective than individual professional judgement and explores some social work practice scenarios that have group decision-making at their core.

The anatomy of making a decision

What is a decision and how do we make one? Let's look at this in very simplistic terms, considering all aspects of the individual and how they interact to reach an end point. At the *beginning*, a decision needs to be made, and this often needs to be assigned to an individual or a group to make. Let's take the example of a parent needing to make a decision about which school their child will attend.

1. *Input.* This will often start as a thought in the mind and a weighing up of information that already exists for the parent to consider.

2. *Information-gathering.* Next, the parent will need to take action and move away from what they already think they know about the options. Small or large amounts of information will need to be gathered from different sources. In this case, these can be from the schools themselves, from word of mouth, reviews and the parent's own existing frame of reference (or in some cases assumptions) that they already have.

3. *Decision point.* Some may think a decision is merely a matter of choosing the best option from the information that has been gathered – and to an extent it is. But you now measure this information against your personal values, moral compass and belief systems before the final act of 'choosing'.

Key perspectives and concepts on group decision-making

The process of decision-making in critical environments has been well researched across varying fields and settings. Decisions in what may be considered high-risk situations and critical fields are of interest across professions. One example in the financial sector, includes banking where they make decisions on mortgages – although this is based on an AI-powered processing of data to arrive at a decision (eg credit scores and affordability testing). Another example in the medical field includes deciding what procedure a person should have based on symptoms, experience and what the individual wants. In social care, a decision may need to be made concerning whether a child should be removed from the care of their parent based on safeguarding thresholds. In politics/conflict situations, decisions are made around national security and the enforcement of a countrywide curfew. For fire personnel, there needs to be an understanding of the different types of fires and how to tackle each one.

But what is the anatomy of each of these decisions and how does an individual or professional make a decision about the next course of action? Research on decision-making in social work has focused its attention on the decisions that individuals make based on their professional judgements, with less attention paid to group decision-making (Alfandari et al, 2023).

To understand collective decision-making, it is important to have some knowledge of key theoretical concepts and approaches. Stemming from psychology, decision-making and groups are joined by cognitive processes and understanding of human interaction and behaviours in groups. The question posed is whether individual decision-making is more effective than group decision-making for service-users and the organisation as a whole (Kerr and Tindale, 2004; Levine et al, 1993). We must present a variety of theoretical perspectives from several disciplines, encompassing various psychological and sociological aspects that could be helpful for professionals working in child and family social work to understand and provide guidance on group decision-making. Human behaviour, interaction and the interest in decision-making are of importance, particularly in a children and families setting, as they are fundamental aspects of practice where decisions are made on a daily basis. In practice, there are key decision-making points for an individual and for their managers (Harvey and Weekes, 2023; Alfandari et al, 2023).

Definition of a group

A group can be defined as an operating collective with the authority to decide or recommend actions to a decision-making individual or body, such as a court. This covers both in-person gatherings and cross-organisational cooperative teams that use a variety of communication channels. Group decision-making is commonly defined as the process of selecting the best alternative(s) among a viable set of possibilities, taking into account the opinions of a group of people who are occasionally referred to as 'experts'. To make decisions as a group, the individual members combine their individual judgements with the goal of arriving at a consensus before collaborating to choose an agreed-upon path of action. Each individual has their own set of knowledge and abilities, or *'professional judgement'* (Alfandari et al, 2023, p 204).

Historically, small groups have been studied in empirical psychological research fragmentally without a unifying theoretical framework. There is a sharp distinction between sub-disciplines (organisational, cognitive and social psychology) in relation to topics investigated and the way groups are viewed. Organisational psychology covers team research, focusing on long-term groups with multiple responsibilities, often within an organisation. Researchers often view teams as complex and dynamic systems, investigate issues such as trust development, roles and interaction patterns, and generate applied knowledge.

Cognitive psychology focuses on the individual's mental activity, viewing group interaction as a stimulus that affects people's mental work. Studies show that the mere presence of other people can influence or impede cognition, such as the phenomenon of 'social loafing'. Another common line of studies investigates the effects of individuals' perceptions about groups on their performance.

In social psychology, the unit of investigation is the whole group, with individuals considered contributors to the group's performance or consensus choice. Traditionally, social psychology adopted an individual-into-group approach and applied individual-level cognitive models to the analysis of group processes. This tendency can be seen in studies of whether groups exacerbate or attenuate individual decision biases, the role of mental models in coordinating group members' activities and systematic measures of group intelligence.

The literature in social psychology is divided into two broad research areas: *group performance* (productivity, problem-solving, creativity tasks) and *group decision-making* (collective selection of a response from a fixed set of alternatives). The *'preference-aggregation paradigm'*, which focuses on how group members combine their preferences into one choice, has evolved over time. Groups may produce better or poorer performances and choices relative to individuals working alone, depending on the context in which group processes occur (Abelson and Levi, 1985).

A common theme that has occupied psychologists through the years relates to the question of whether numerous heads are more effective than one, which seems to have no easy answer (Kerr and Tindale, 2004; Levine et al, 1993). Corporations may additionally produce higher or poorer performances and alternatives relative to people working on their own, relying on the context wherein institution approaches occur – for example, whether or not the institution motivates the investment in extra effort (Larson, 2010).

Group consensus processes

In the past, research on majority and minority influences in groups focused on how disagreements among individuals can affect their thoughts, while ignoring the explicit pressure for group members to reach a shared decision (Levine et al, 1993). Janis's (1971) groundbreaking research in the early 1970s provided a unique analysis. He demonstrated that group decision-making can lead to suboptimal decisions due to the phenomenon of *'groupthink'*, which he defined as the tendency for groups to make decisions based on a desire for conformity and avoidance of disagreement. Janis used this concept to explain significant events in US foreign policy history, such as the Bay of Pigs fiasco and the Cuban missile crisis. Groupthink is characterised by the following core signs.

» Group members unquestioningly believe in the inherent morality of their own group and feel invulnerable.

» Warnings and negative feedback are rationalised, and people outside the group are ignored or demonised, often by self-appointed censors or 'mind guards'.

» Group members feel pressured by the group or by self-censorship to remain silent about their doubts, especially to outsiders.

» Decisions are marked by an illusion of unanimity, assuming that silence implies agreement with what is being said (Janis, 1971).

Janis's model is valuable because it offers several strategies to counteract groupthink. These include leaders initially refraining from stating their views, actively encouraging different perspectives, involving external experts and allowing lower-ranking members of the group to speak first (Janis, 1971, 1982).

In the field of psychology, the social identity approach presents a broader perspective on group decision-making compared with the limited groupthink model. While groupthink focuses on situations where decision-making is flawed, social identity analysis suggests the changes that occur during collective decision-making are rational psychological processes based on the essence of the group, efficient from a psychological standpoint, grounded in the social reality experienced by group members and with the potential to positively impact society (Larson, 2010).

When it comes to formal systems of decision-making, there are two main approaches: *consensus decision-making* (Bressen, 2007) and the *voting-based method* (Cheng and Deek, 2012) (such as the child protection conference that uses the voting model).

Consensus decision-making aims to avoid creating 'winners' and 'losers'. It requires a majority of the group to approve a particular course of action, while also ensuring that the minority agrees to go along with it. If the minority opposes the proposed course of action, consensus dictates that modifications should be made to address their concerns.

On the other hand, voting-based methods involve different approaches. Range voting allows each member to assign scores to one or more available options, with the option that has the highest average score chosen. This method has been experimentally proven to produce the lowest Bayesian regret among common voting methods, even when voters strategically manipulate their scores.

Majority decision-making, as the name suggests, requires support from more than 50 per cent of the group members. This means the threshold for taking action is lower compared with unanimity. However, it is important to note that this approach inherently implies the existence of a group of 'losers' who did not support the chosen course of action. Another approach is plurality, where the decision is made by the largest bloc in the group, even if it does not constitute a majority.

The examination of decision-making in groups often involves analysing both the process and the outcome separately. The process refers to the interactions within the group, including the formation of coalitions, the use of influence and persuasion, and the involvement of politics. Although the use of politics is often viewed negatively, it can be a valuable approach when there are conflicting preferences among group members, unavoidable dependencies or the absence of higher authorities, or when the technical or scientific merit of options is unclear (Housley, 2003).

Apart from the various processes involved in decision-making, group decision-support systems (GDSSs) can also have different decision rules. A decision rule in a GDSS is the protocol or guideline that a group follows to select among alternative scenarios in scenario planning.

One approach is gathering, which involves all participants acknowledging each other's needs and opinions. This approach aims to find a problem-solving solution that satisfies as many needs and opinions as possible. It allows for multiple outcomes and does not require unanimous agreement for action to be taken – if we think about this in relation to social work practice, we may think of fostering and adoption panels.

Another approach is the use of sub-committees, where a sub-set of the larger group is assigned the responsibility of evaluating a decision and then presenting recommendations to the larger group. Sub-committees are more commonly used in larger governance groups, such as legislatures. In some cases the sub-committee includes individuals who are most affected by the decision, while in other cases it may involve more neutral participants to provide a balanced perspective (Haslam, 2004).

At times, groups may have established and clearly defined standards for decision-making, such as bylaws and statutes. However, it is common for the decision-making process to be less formal and it may even be implicitly accepted. Social decision schemes refer to the methods employed by a group to combine individual responses and arrive at a single group decision. There are several of these schemes, but the following are the most prevalent.

1. *Delegation*. In this scheme, an individual, sub-group or external party makes the decision on behalf of the entire group. For example, in an authority scheme, the leader takes charge of making the decision, or in an oligarchy, a coalition of prominent figures makes the decision.
2. *Averaging*. Each member of the group independently makes their own private decision, and these individual decisions are later 'averaged' to generate a collective decision.
3. *Plurality*. Group members vote on their preferences, either privately or publicly. These votes are then utilised to select a decision, which can be determined by a simple majority, supermajority or other more complex voting system.
4. *Unanimity*. This scheme involves a consensus approach where the group engages in discussions until they reach a unanimous agreement. This decision rule is commonly employed in the decision-making process for most juries (Hastie and Kameda, 2005).

Each of these social decision schemes has its strengths and weaknesses. Delegation saves time and works well for less-important decisions, but it may result in negative reactions from ignored members. Averaging responses helps to balance extreme opinions, but the final decision may disappoint many members. Plurality is the most consistent scheme for making superior decisions and requires the least effort. However, voting can make members feel alienated if they lose a close vote, or it may lead to internal politics and conformity to other opinions. Consensus schemes involve members more deeply and often result in high levels of commitment. However, reaching such decisions may be challenging for the group.

The normative model of decision-making encompasses various approaches that leaders can adopt when making decisions in a group setting. These approaches consider the advantages and disadvantages of group decision-making (Vroom, 2003).

One approach is the *decide method*, where the leader independently makes the final decision after gathering information from group members without explaining the rationale behind it. Another is the *consult (individual) method*, where the leader individually consults each group member and considers their input before making the final decision. The *consult (group) method* involves the leader convening a group meeting and seeking opinions and information from all members before arriving at a decision (Forsyth, 2006; Vroom, 2003).

In the *facilitate method*, the leader adopts a cooperative and inclusive approach, collaborating with the group as a whole to reach a unified and consensual decision. The leader does not impose a specific solution on the group and the final decision is made collectively (Forsyth, 2006; Vroom, 2003).

Lastly, the *delegate method* involves the leader taking a more hands-off approach, allowing the group to independently reach a decision without direct collaboration. The leader provides support but does not actively participate in the decision-making process. By understanding these different decision-making processes, leaders can select the most appropriate approach based on the specific situation at hand (Forsyth, 2006; Vroom, 2003).

Decision support systems

James Reason (1990) explores the concept of intelligent decision support systems in his research on human error, focusing specifically on the use of computerised support systems. However, Reason acknowledges that certain incidents, such as the Davis-Besse accident, have raised doubts about the effectiveness of these methods. In this particular accident, both independent safety parameter display systems were non-functional before and during the event.

Autonomous robots and various forms of active decision support for industrial operators, designers and managers rely heavily on decision-making software. Given the complexity of many decisions, computer-based decision support systems (DSS) have been developed to assist decision-makers in evaluating the consequences of different thought processes. These systems play a crucial role in minimising the risk of human error. DSSs that aim to replicate human cognitive decision-making functions are referred to as Intelligent Decision Support Systems (IDSS). Conversely, an active and intelligent DSS serves as a vital tool in the design of intricate engineering systems and the management of large-scale technological and business projects.

Groups possess greater informational and motivational resources, which gives them the potential to surpass individuals in performance. However, this potential is not always realised. One of the main reasons for this is the lack of proper communication skills within groups. On one hand, group members may struggle to express themselves clearly, hindering effective communication. On the other hand, miscommunication can occur due to limitations in information processing and faulty listening habits among individuals. Additionally, when an individual holds control over the group, it can prevent others from making meaningful contributions.

Furthermore, groups sometimes resort to using discussions as a means to avoid making decisions. This avoidance can take various forms, including *procrastination*, where the group postpones decision-making by replacing high-priority tasks with lower-priority ones. Another tactic is *bolstering*, where the group hastily formulates a decision without thorough consideration, then tries to strengthen it by exaggerating the positive outcomes and downplaying the negative consequences.

Denying responsibility is another tactic, where the group delegates the decision to a sub-committee or spreads accountability across the entire group to evade taking responsibility. Muddling through is yet another tactic, where the group only considers a narrow range of alternatives that differ minimally from the existing choice, thus failing to explore more viable options. *Satisficing* is a term coined by combining 'satisfy' and 'suffice', and it refers to the group's tendency to accept a low-risk, easy solution instead of actively searching for the best possible solution (Schwartz et al, 2010).

In summary, groups often adhere to two fundamental 'laws' that hinder their potential: the lack of effective communication skills and the tendency to use discussion as a means of avoidance.

Parkinson's law states that a task will expand to occupy the entire time allotted for its completion. In other words, if there is a deadline for a task, people tend to take up all the available time to finish it, regardless of the actual amount of work required. This law highlights the tendency for work to expand and fill the time given, leading to potential inefficiencies and delays (Kilmeck et al, 2009).

On the other hand, the *law of triviality* suggests that the amount of time spent discussing an issue within a group is often disproportionate to its importance or impact. For instance, a committee may spend only a few minutes discussing a significant expenditure of £20 million, while dedicating a much longer time to debating a relatively minor expense of £500. This phenomenon occurs due to the tendency of individuals to focus on trivial matters that are easier to comprehend and discuss rather than tackling more complex or consequential issues (Lu et al, 2011; Reason, 1990; Stasser and Williams, 1985).

Moreover, research on group decision-making has revealed the problem of failure to share information. In situations where certain group members possess information that is unknown to others, the overall decision-making process can be compromised. If all members were to share their information, the group would have a higher likelihood of making an optimal decision. However, when individuals withhold or only partially share their information, the group may end up making suboptimal choices. Studies have demonstrated that partial sharing of information can lead to incorrect decisions, emphasising the importance of open and comprehensive information-sharing within a group. In fact, research has shown that groups are significantly more likely to answer a problem correctly when all members possess all the relevant information, compared with situations where only select individuals have access to certain information.

Individual versus group decision-making

Studies on social workers' decision-making are often described as being influenced by two contrasting dimensions: rationality and intuition. However, there is no clear boundary between these two dimensions. While managerial decision-making is commonly viewed as a purely rational process, intuition plays a significant role in social workers' decision-making (Sicora et al, 2021). Therefore, it is essential to consider the theoretical framework that guides the decision-making process. Research suggests individuals may rely on stereotypes and personal theories rather than objective data when making judgements. Additionally, once a person's views or decisions are formed, they tend to remain unchanged even if the evidence suggests otherwise (Lord et al, 1979). This highlights the importance of acknowledging and addressing potential biases and preconceived notions in decision-making.

Rational ('rationalisable') decision-making

Abelson and Levi (1985) propose models of decision-making, emphasising the role of structure and process in the rational psychological processes involved in judgement and choice. They argue that individuals must continuously assess and evaluate information to make sound judgements. In situations where there are well-defined problems, decision-makers need to gather and process information about available options before making a choice (Abelson and Levi, 1985, p 255). To avoid the influence of confirmation bias, it is believed that decision-makers should regularly challenge their assumptions by actively seeking out information that may contradict them (O'Sullivan, 2011). De Bortoli and Dolan (2015) stress the importance of combining professional judgement with empirical elements in the decision-making process to enhance cognitive processes. Additionally, Resnik (2002) acknowledges that decisions involve three key components: actions or non-actions taken; factors influencing these decisions; and uncertainty regarding outcomes. A thorough approach informed by both professional expertise and empirical evidence is therefore crucial for effective decision-making (Weekes, 2020; Harvey and Weekes, 2023).

Intuitive decision-making

Intuition is a cognitive process that can result in an answer, solution or idea without following a conscious, logical step-by-step approach (Hammond, 1996). It has attracted interest in the decision-making process in recent years with several studies exploring the role of intuition in managerial decision-making (Sicora et al, 2021; Simon, 1987). However, some argue that intuition is a problematic concept as it does not abide by any standard or definitive rule (Kahneman, 2011). This highlights how we often rely on intuition even in unpredictable situations.

Decision-making within the social work context

The focus of this chapter has been decision-making in groups within the social work practice setting.

Can you think of circumstances when a decision needs to be made in a group within social work? The following is a list of examples – can you think of any others?

- » Family group conference.
- » Child protection conference.
- » CIN (child in need) meeting.
- » Adoption and fostering panels.
- » Funding panel.
- » MDTs (multidisciplinary teams) in hospitals.
- » Youth justice panel meetings.

The systemic unit models, also known as 'reclaiming social work' or the 'Hackney model' (Forrester et al, 2013), were developed to facilitate a comprehensive approach to managing cases within a team. Utilising systemic principles and techniques, the model placed a strong emphasis on family therapy and involved a select group of practitioners. While its effectiveness in reducing risk has received mixed reviews, valuable insights have been gained from it. As a result, local authorities' children's services departments have adopted similar safeguarding models that prioritise family involvement and offer specialised assistance for individuals dealing with substance misuse, domestic abuse and mental health challenges. This necessitates social workers possessing 'strong collaborative skills in order to effectively collaborate with various professionals' (Haughton et al, 2023).

Key challenges

Managing emotions within decision-making processes

Effective decision-making in social care is crucial for promoting accountability and justifying the rationale behind decisions. Various theories of management decision-making, including those from psychology, business and healthcare perspectives, have been discussed extensively in the literature (Bakay et al, 2014; Hsu, 2014; Johnston and Paulsen, 2014; Sen et al, 2011; Shi et al, 2015; Simon, 1992). To better understand the process of making sound decisions in social work, two psychoanalytical concepts can be applied: Winnicott's (1953, 1971) concept of *'holding'* and Bion's (1962) concept of *'container–contained'*. While these terms are often used interchangeably, they are distinct and should not be conflated. Together, they potentially provide a comprehensive understanding of the caregiver's ability to provide emotional support and meet the needs of their child, both physically and symbolically (Weekes, 2020).

> **Case study**
>
> **Connor**
>
> Connor is 15 years old and is in trouble with the police. Connor was caught on a stolen moped and arrested in the early hours of the morning on a school night. He is currently at the police station. This is the first time he has been arrested.

> ### Reflective exercise
>
> After reading the above case study, do the following:
> » List the professionals that need to make a decision.
> » Identify the point at which they will need to make a decision.
> » Identify whether a group decision or an individual decision needs to be made (to stretch yourself, identify which group decision-making model is being used).
>
> Capture personal reflections and individual thoughts
> » Critically reflect on this chapter so far and what you have learned, and record your own personal thoughts and feelings.

Chapter summary

This chapter has explored whether decisions are best made in a group or by an individual. It has looked at the theoretical basis for group decision-making and applied this to the group decision-making process within social work practice.

For years, responsibility for a case has always been held by the social worker – media headlines like those related to Victoria Climbié (Laming, 2003) highlight social workers' failings regarding acting and making decisions. Group thinking and decision-making came to the fore post the *Children Act 2004*, where there was more accountability for professionals sharing information and making safeguarding everyone's responsibility. Known to over ten professional services including police, hospital, social care and housing departments, in the inquiry report Neil Garnham QC states that the opportunities to intervene were many:

> *Not one of these required great skill or would have made heavy demands on time to take some form of action. Sometimes it needed nothing more than a manager doing their job by asking pertinent questions or taking the trouble to look in a case file. There can be no excuse for such sloppy and unprofessional performance.*
>
> (Laming, 2003, p 15)

> *Even after listening to all the evidence, I remain amazed that nobody in any of the key agencies had the presence of mind to follow what are relatively straightforward procedures on how to respond to a child about whom there is concern of deliberate harm.*
>
> (Laming, 2003, p 16)

Citing management malaise for the poor decision-making and action, Lord Laming adds:

> *The greatest failure rests with the managers and senior members of the authorities whose task it was to ensure that services for children, like Victoria, were properly financed, staffed, and able to deliver good quality support to children and families. It is significant that while a number of junior staff in Haringey Social Services were suspended and faced disciplinary action after Victoria's death, some of their most senior officers were being appointed to other, presumably better paid, jobs.*
>
> (Laming, 2003, p 16)

Now we have a more collective measure in thinking about risk and making individual and group decisions. Child protection conferences collectively review concerns, look at risk and assess what is working well. They hold professionals accountable as part of a plan to keep a child or young person from harm.

Family network meetings empower families to consider all possible support within the family of who is best placed to care for a child or young person. Foster and adoption panels consider information gathered in a full assessment and make decisions about who is suitable to foster or adopt. More rigorous processes have allowed group thinking in decisions and accountability. While this may seem a more progressive and positive step forward, does it take away the autonomy of individual professionals in decision-making? After all, social workers are trained for between two and three years to be able to practise in real-life situations. Do professionals get stuck between rational and intuitive decision-making states (Abelson and Levi, 1985)? Important decisions are often made by groups that have more experience, increased processing capabilities and the ability to monitor each other for mistakes and share information regarding the task and the expected behaviours of others. Therefore, groups mostly act more rationally than in an intuitive or selfish way, which means their behaviour is more in line with the theoretical concepts.

Key takeaways from this chapter

- *Shift from individual to group accountability.* Historically, individual social workers were solely accountable for case decisions, which often led to blame in high-profile failures (eg the Victoria Climbié case). The *Children Act 2004* shifted the focus towards collective responsibility, promoting multi-agency collaboration in safeguarding children. However, this needs to be set within the context of individual responsibilities.

- *Advantages of group decision-making.* Group decision-making in social work – through mechanisms such as child protection conferences and foster panels – brings diverse perspectives, greater scrutiny and shared accountability, leading to more thorough risk assessments and protective measures.

- *Management failures highlighted.* The Victoria Climbié inquiry pointed to systemic management failures, where senior leaders avoided accountability despite significant oversights, leaving frontline staff to face disciplinary actions. This underscores the need for better management oversight in social work.

- *Tension between autonomy and group consensus.* While group decision-making offers benefits such as reducing individual bias, it may also limit the professional autonomy of social workers. Social workers may feel constrained in using their judgement, leading to potential decision paralysis or over-reliance on group norms.

- *Balancing rational and intuitive judgement.* Social workers are trained to navigate both rational and intuitive decision-making. The challenge is to balance the strengths of group processes with the need for individual professional judgement, ensuring that decisions are both comprehensive and contextually appropriate.

Chapter 7 | Applying EPPJ

I would like to be remembered as a person who wanted to be free ... so other people would also be free.

Rosa Parks (1990)

Introduction

Effective Personal and Professional Judgement (EPPJ) is a concept that has gained increasing importance in the realms of personal development, organisational leadership and decision-making processes. At its core, EPPJ embodies the capacity to make sound, well-reasoned decisions that are aligned with both personal values and professional standards. This chapter delves into the foundational research that underpins EPPJ, exploring its theoretical origins, the key factors that influence it, and its application in various contexts. The chapter also examines the interplay between personal and professional judgement, highlighting the ethical, cognitive and emotional dimensions that shape EPPJ.

Understanding key terms in anti-oppression and social justice work

To navigate and understand the complexities of oppression, inequality and discrimination, it is essential to define key terms that have emerged from critical theory and social justice scholarship. This chapter explores six foundational concepts: misogynoir, intersectionality, adultification, institutional racism, structural racism, and internalised oppression, linking them to EPPJ. Through these definitions, we can better understand how these forms of oppression manifest, how they intersect, and the importance of reflective practice in challenging them.

Misogynoir (Bailey)

Coined by Moya Bailey, the term misogynoir refers to the specific intersection of misogyny and racism that is directed at Black women. Misogynoir illuminates the compounded forms of discrimination that Black women face, which cannot be fully explained by sexism or racism alone. Bailey's concept (Bailey, 2010) critiques the ways Black women are hypersexualised, dehumanised and neglected in both the media and societal structures. This term emerged to fill a gap in the discourse on the unique experiences of Black women who navigate both gendered and racial oppression simultaneously.

Misogynoir is a pervasive phenomenon that manifests in stereotypes such as the 'angry Black woman' or the hypersexualised 'Jezebel', which serve to justify the mistreatment of Black women in both private and public spheres. The representation of Black women in media often reflects these harmful stereotypes, perpetuating a cycle of discrimination that influences how Black women are treated in real life. Understanding misogynoir is critical to addressing the nuanced challenges faced by Black women and is essential for dismantling both racist and sexist systems.

Intersectionality (Crenshaw)

Kimberlé Crenshaw's concept of intersectionality has become foundational in understanding how different forms of discrimination overlap and intersect in the lives of individuals. Originally developed in the context of Black feminist thought, intersectionality highlights how categories such as race, gender, class and sexuality are interconnected and cannot be examined in isolation. Crenshaw (1989) used the example of Black women's experiences to demonstrate how existing anti-discrimination laws and feminist theory often failed to capture the complexity of their lived realities.

Intersectionality is not merely about adding up different forms of oppression but about recognising that these forms of discrimination work together to produce unique experiences. For example, a Black woman may experience discrimination in a way that is qualitatively different from both Black men and white women. Intersectionality challenges the notion of a singular or monolithic experience of oppression and instead argues for a more nuanced understanding of how systems of power interact. In doing so, it provides a critical lens through which to analyse both individual and institutional behaviour, making it indispensable in social justice work.

Adultification (Davies)

Adultification refers to the process by which Black children, particularly girls, are perceived as older and less innocent than their white counterparts, leading to disproportionate and often harsher treatment. Scholars such as Angela J H Davies have examined this concept, arguing that Black children are often viewed through an adult lens, which strips them of the protective qualities typically associated with childhood (Davies, 2018). This perception leads to increased surveillance, harsher disciplinary measures in schools and, in some cases, unjust encounters with law enforcement.

Adultification is deeply rooted in historical stereotypes about Black people, which portray them as inherently more resilient or more mature than white people. This distorted perception has long-lasting consequences for Black children, who are denied the opportunity to make mistakes, learn and grow in the same ways that their white peers can. Research has shown that Black girls are often seen as more knowledgeable about adult topics, such as sex, and are less likely to receive empathy or leniency. By understanding adultification, we can better address the systemic biases that contribute to the disproportionate punishment and criminalisation of Black children.

Institutional racism (Carmichael and Hamilton; Macpherson)

Institutional racism refers to the systemic policies and practices within institutions that create and perpetuate racial inequalities, often without explicit intent. This concept was introduced by Stokely Carmichael and Charles V Hamilton (1967) in *Black Power: The Politics of Liberation*, where they argued that racism is embedded in the policies and procedures of societal institutions, making it a pervasive force that does not rely on individual acts of prejudice.

The 1999 Macpherson Report, produced after the murder of Stephen Lawrence, expanded on this concept, defining institutional racism as *'the collective failure of an organisation to provide an appropriate and professional service to people because of their colour, culture, or ethnic origin'* (Macpherson, 1999). Macpherson's definition highlights how institutional racism operates through unwitting prejudice, ignorance and stereotyping, which result in discriminatory outcomes. Examples of institutional racism can be found in the education system, the criminal justice system, healthcare and employment practices, where people of colour are disproportionately disadvantaged. Addressing institutional racism requires not only changes in policies but also a shift in the culture and practices of institutions.

Structural racism (Miller)

Structural racism refers to the overarching system of racial inequality that is embedded within society's major institutions, policies and social structures. It goes beyond individual or institutional racism to examine how historical and societal factors, such as colonialism, slavery and segregation, have created deep-rooted disparities in wealth, health, education and opportunities. Structural racism manifests through cumulative disadvantages that are passed down through the generations, resulting in a persistent racial hierarchy (Miller, 2021).

For example, the racial wealth gap in countries like the United States and the United Kingdom is a product of structural racism, wherein systemic barriers such as discriminatory housing policies, exclusion from quality education and unequal access to healthcare perpetuate economic and social inequality. Structural racism cannot be dismantled through individual action alone; it requires a collective effort to reimagine and restructure societal systems. Only by addressing these ingrained inequalities at a structural level can true racial equity be achieved.

Philosophical foundations for social work practice and the decision-making EPPJ model

In the context of social work, decision-making is influenced not only by policy, law and ethics but also by broader philosophical ideas that shape our understanding of humanity, power, communication and development. Various philosophical theories offer frameworks for understanding human behaviour, justice and interpersonal relationships. In this chapter, we will explore the contributions of key thinkers Ludwig Wittgenstein, Paolo Freire, Socrates, Ptah-Hotep, John Dewey, Frantz Fanon, Henry Odera Oruka, Friedrich Nietzsche, Mogobe Bernard Ramos and Erik Erikson by comparing and contrasting their ideas. The EPPJ model emphasises self-awareness, reflection and ethical action in decision-making processes.

Language and social work practice

Ludwig Wittgenstein's (1953) philosophy of language, particularly in his later work, emphasises how language is embedded in forms of life, meaning our understanding of the world is shaped by how we use language in social contexts. In social work, language is a powerful tool not only for communication but also for framing clients' problems and potential solutions. Wittgenstein's emphasis on the *'meaning of language'* being determined by its use implies that how social workers speak with clients, colleagues and communities shapes their understanding of the world.

In the context of social work, this theory can be linked to the EPPJ model, particularly in fostering self-awareness and reflection on how language is used within practice. The language professionals use can either empower or disempower clients. For example, describing a client as 'challenging' may lead to a more negative and reductive interpretation of their behaviour, reinforcing existing biases. Wittgenstein's insights prompt social workers to critically evaluate how language shapes their judgements and decision-making, ensuring it aligns with anti-oppressive practice.

Liberation pedagogy and empowerment

Paulo Freire's (1970) theory of liberation pedagogy offers a revolutionary approach to education, premised on dialogue, empowerment and the recognition of oppressed people's capacity for self-liberation. Freire critiques traditional models of education as *'banking systems'* where knowledge is deposited into passive learners. Instead, he advocates for education that is dialogical, allowing individuals to co-create knowledge and thereby liberate themselves from oppression.

In social work, Freire's ideas underpin approaches that emphasise client empowerment, participation and self-determination. Rather than positioning the social worker as an expert imposing a solution, a Freirean approach involves working alongside clients, encouraging them to find their own pathways to change. The EPPJ model emphasises the importance of reflection and critical consciousness. Like Freire's pedagogy, it urges practitioners to challenge power dynamics and work in ways that promote the agency and empowerment of clients, thus aligning social work with anti-oppressive practice.

Dialectic and critical thinking

Socrates' method of dialectic, or dialogue, involves asking probing questions to stimulate critical thinking and uncover deeper truths. His emphasis on questioning and dialogue is foundational to many forms of inquiry, including the practice of social work. Social workers often use questioning to help clients explore their thoughts, behaviours and emotions, facilitating self-discovery and empowerment. The Socratic method complements the EPPJ model's focus on reflection and critical self-awareness. In social work decision-making, dialectical inquiry allows for deeper understanding and helps avoid snap judgements or assumptions. By engaging in dialogue with clients, colleagues and themselves, social workers can challenge biases and consider multiple perspectives, leading to more informed and ethical decisions.

Active listening and ethical leadership

Ancient Egyptian philosopher Ptah-Hotep (c. 2400 BCE) emphasised active listening as a key component of effective communication and ethical leadership. He believed that listening carefully to others was a sign of wisdom and respect, allowing for more thoughtful and fair decision-making. This principle is central to effective social work practice, where listening is crucial to understanding the lived experiences of clients, especially those from marginalised or oppressed backgrounds. Active listening within the EPPJ model, particularly in its emphasis on ethical action and professional judgement, plays a central role. Social workers who practise active listening are better equipped to make decisions that are truly responsive to the needs and desires of their clients, thereby supporting empowerment and self-determination.

Pragmatism and reflective practice

John Dewey's pragmatism focuses on the practical consequences of ideas and decisions, arguing that knowledge and truth are not static but instead evolve through experience and action (Dewey, 1938). Dewey's concept of reflective practice has profound implications for social work. It emphasises the need for continuous reflection and adaptation, particularly considering the changing needs of clients and communities. Dewey's pragmatism directly informs the EPPJ model's emphasis on reflection as a principal component of ethical decision-making. Like Dewey, EPPJ argues that professionals must continuously reflect on their actions and adjust their approaches to better serve clients. Pragmatism encourages a flexible, open-minded approach, where professionals are willing to revise their strategies based on new evidence or understanding, ensuring more responsive and ethical practice.

Liberation and decolonisation

Frantz Fanon's (1961) work on liberation and decolonisation offers a powerful critique of colonialism and its psychological effects on both the colonised and colonisers. His analysis of racial oppression and the internalisation of inferiority has particular relevance for social work, especially in addressing systemic inequalities and promoting social justice. Fanon's theories challenge social workers to consider the historical and structural forces that shape the experiences of marginalised groups. His ideas resonate through the EPPJ model's focus on critical consciousness, urging professionals to recognise and challenge the ways their practice may be complicit in maintaining systems of oppression. In line with Fanon's liberation philosophy, social workers are encouraged to act as agents of change, advocating for systemic reform while empowering individuals and communities.

Philosophic sagacity

Henry Odera Oruka's concept of philosophic sagacity refers to the wisdom of African sages who, while often not formally educated, possess deep philosophical insight into human behaviour and society (Oruka, 1990). This emphasis on Indigenous knowledge systems challenges the dominance of Western philosophical traditions and highlights the importance of culturally relevant approaches to understanding and decision-making. In social work, recognising philosophic sagacity can promote culturally competent practice. The EPPJ model encourages social workers to engage in reflective practice that is sensitive to the cultural contexts of their clients. By valuing diverse sources of knowledge, including those rooted in Indigenous traditions, social workers can make more inclusive and respectful decisions.

Power and ethics

Friedrich Nietzsche's (1883) philosophy often centres around the concept of power, particularly the will to power as a driving force in human behaviour. Nietzsche's ideas challenge traditional moral frameworks, advocating for individuals to create their own values and reject societal norms that suppress human potential. In social work, Nietzsche's philosophy invites critical reflection on the role of power in professional relationships. While Nietzsche's individualistic approach may seem at odds with the profession's emphasis on collective well-being, his focus on power dynamics aligns with the EPPJ model's critical consciousness component. Social workers must be aware of how power operates within their practice and strive to create more egalitarian and empowering relationships with their clients.

Ubuntu and community

Mogobe Bernard Ramose's (1999) philosophy of Ubuntu emphasises the interconnectedness of all people, captured in the phrase 'I am because we are'. Ubuntu focuses on communal relationships, mutual care and the idea that one's humanity is inextricably linked to the well-being of others. This philosophy deeply resonates with the values of social work, particularly in fostering a sense of collective responsibility and social solidarity. The EPPJ model aligns with Ubuntu's emphasis on ethical action as it prioritises the collective good and promotes decisions made in the interest of community well-being. In social work, Ubuntu encourages a holistic approach to practice, where the needs of the individual are understood within the context of their community.

Psychosocial development

Erik Erikson's (1950) psychosocial development theory outlines the stages of human development, each marked by a specific conflict that must be resolved for healthy psychological growth. This theory provides a valuable framework for social workers in terms of understanding clients' developmental challenges, particularly in relation to identity-formation, autonomy and relationships. Erikson's theory complements the EPPJ model's focus on reflection as it encourages social workers to consider how clients' developmental stages influence their behaviour and needs. Understanding these stages can inform more empathetic and effective interventions, ensuring that social workers make decisions that are developmentally appropriate and supportive of clients' growth.

Each of these philosophical perspectives offers valuable insights into social work practice and decision-making: Wittgenstein's focus on language, Freire's liberation pedagogy, Socrates' dialectical method, Ptah-Hotep's active listening, Dewey's pragmatism, Fanon's liberation philosophy, Oruka's philosophic sagacity, Nietzsche's power dynamics, Ramose's Ubuntu and Erikson's psychosocial development all provide distinct but complementary frameworks for understanding the complexities of human behaviour, power and justice. When applied to social work, these ideas support a more reflective, ethical and socially conscious practice, closely aligned with the principles of the EPPJ model. Through ongoing reflection, critical consciousness and ethical action, social workers can make decisions that are not only effective but also grounded in a commitment to social justice and human dignity.

Theoretical foundations

The concept of judgement has been a subject of philosophical inquiry for centuries. Classical philosophers such as Aristotle, Kant and Mill have all grappled with the nature of judgement, ethics and decision-making. Aristotle's notion of phronesis, or practical wisdom, is particularly relevant to EPPJ. Phronesis involves the ability to deliberate effectively about what is good and beneficial for oneself and for others in the context of a well-lived life. Aristotle emphasised that phronesis is not just theoretical knowledge (episteme) or technical skill (techne), but a virtue that requires experience, moral character and the ability to apply knowledge in real-world situations.

In the modern era, the concept of judgement has been refined further by cognitive psychology, which investigates the processes by which individuals make decisions. The dual-process theory, which distinguishes between intuitive (System 1) and analytical (System 2) thinking, provides a valuable framework for understanding EPPJ. System 1 is fast, automatic and often relies on heuristics, whereas System 2 is slower, deliberate and analytical. Effective judgement, whether personal or professional, often involves a balance between these two systems, where intuition is informed by experience and analysis.

Ethical theories, particularly deontology and consequentialism, also play a critical role in shaping EPPJ. Deontological ethics, as articulated by Immanuel Kant, posits that actions should be judged based on adherence to rules or duties, regardless of the outcomes. In contrast, consequentialism – particularly utilitarianism as espoused by Jeremy Bentham and John Stuart Mill (2007) – evaluates actions based on the consequences they produce, aiming for the greatest good for the greatest number. EPPJ often requires navigating the tension between these ethical frameworks, particularly in professional contexts where decisions may impact a wide range of stakeholders.

Key factors influencing EPPJ

Several factors influence the effectiveness of personal and professional judgement. These can broadly be categorised into cognitive, emotional, ethical and contextual dimensions.

Cognitive factors

Cognitive factors are central to EPPJ, as they involve the mental processes by which individuals perceive, process and evaluate information. Critical thinking is one of the most important cognitive skills for effective judgement. It involves the ability to analyse arguments, identify logical fallacies and synthesise information from multiple sources. Critical thinking is particularly crucial in professional settings, where decisions often need to be made based on incomplete or ambiguous information.

Cognitive biases, such as confirmation bias, anchoring and over-confidence, can significantly impair judgement. Confirmation bias, the tendency to search for or interpret information in a way that confirms one's preconceptions, can lead to flawed decisions. Anchoring, the tendency to rely too heavily on the first piece of information encountered, can skew judgement, particularly in situations where accurate forecasting or assessment is required. Over-confidence, the tendency to over-estimate one's knowledge or abilities, can result in overly risky decisions or the dismissal of alternative perspectives. Developing awareness of these biases is a critical component of enhancing EPPJ.

Emotional factors

Emotions play a complex role in decision-making and judgement. While emotions can sometimes cloud judgement, leading to impulsive or irrational decisions, they can also provide valuable insights and motivation. Emotional intelligence, which involves the ability to recognise, understand and manage one's own emotions as well as the emotions of others, is essential for effective judgement. High emotional intelligence enables individuals to navigate social dynamics, empathise with others and make decisions that are not only rational but also emotionally resonant.

Stress and anxiety can negatively impact judgement by narrowing focus and reducing cognitive flexibility. Under conditions of high stress, individuals are more likely to rely on heuristics or default responses rather than engaging in thoughtful deliberation. However, moderate levels of stress can sometimes enhance performance by sharpening focus and motivation, a phenomenon known as the Yerkes–Dodson Law. Therefore, effective management of stress and emotions is crucial for maintaining sound judgement in both personal and professional contexts.

Ethical factors

Ethical considerations are at the heart of EPPJ, particularly in professional settings where decisions often have significant moral implications. Ethical judgement involves not only adhering to legal and professional standards but also considering broader societal impacts and the welfare of all stakeholders. This requires a well-developed moral compass, which is informed by both personal values and an understanding of ethical principles.

The concept of moral courage is particularly relevant to EPPJ. Moral courage involves the willingness to make complex decisions that may be unpopular or risky but are aligned with one's ethical beliefs. This is especially important in situations where there is pressure to conform to unethical practices or where the right course of action is not immediately clear. Developing moral courage requires a strong sense of personal integrity and the ability to act consistently with one's values, even in the face of adversity.

Contextual factors

Context plays a critical role in shaping judgement. The social, cultural and organisational environment can influence the way individuals perceive and respond to situations. In professional settings, organisational culture and leadership styles can significantly impact judgement. A culture that encourages open communication, critical thinking and ethical behaviour is likely to foster better judgement among its members. Conversely, a culture that prioritises conformity, short-term results or rigid hierarchies may impair judgement by discouraging diverse perspectives and ethical considerations.

Contextual awareness involves understanding the broader environment in which decisions are made, including the social dynamics, power structures and external pressures that may influence judgement. This awareness enables individuals to navigate complex situations more effectively and to anticipate the potential consequences of their decisions.

Internalised oppression and EPPJ

Internalised oppression refers to the process by which individuals from marginalised groups come to accept and believe negative stereotypes and discriminatory messages about their own group. This can lead to feelings of inferiority, self-doubt and behaviours that reinforce oppressive systems. For example, a non-white person may internalise the notion that they are less capable or deserving of success, which can affect their self-esteem and ambitions. Internalised oppression is a psychological consequence of living in a society that constantly reinforces negative messages about one's racial, gender or class identity.

The EPPJ model offers a framework for addressing internalised oppression by promoting self-awareness and critical reflection. EPPJ encourages individuals, particularly professionals, to examine their own biases, attitudes and decisions in the context of broader societal inequalities (Weekes, 2016). By engaging in this reflective practice, individuals can better understand how internalised oppression influences their personal and professional lives and can take steps to challenge and dismantle these internalised beliefs.

EPPJ has a practical application in professional settings, where it helps practitioners avoid making judgements based on stereotypes or internalised biases. For example, in social work, educators who are aware of how internalised oppression affects both themselves and the children with whom they work are better equipped to provide supportive and empowering environments. The EPPJ model highlights the importance of personal reflection in making ethical and effective decisions that challenge oppressive systems, making it a valuable tool for anti-oppressive practice.

Interplay between personal and professional judgement

The distinction between personal and professional judgement is often blurred, as the values, principles and cognitive processes that underpin both are closely intertwined. However, there are also crucial differences in how judgement is applied in personal versus professional contexts.

Personal judgement

Personal judgement is guided primarily by individual values, beliefs and experiences. It involves making decisions that align with one's personal goals and ethical standards. Personal judgement is often influenced by factors such as family, culture and personal history, which shape one's identity and worldview. In personal contexts, judgement is often more intuitive and emotionally driven, reflecting the deep-seated values and preferences of the individual. However, personal judgement is not isolated from professional considerations. For example, decisions about work–life balance, career choices and interpersonal relationships often require balancing personal desires with professional responsibilities. The ability to integrate personal and professional values into a coherent framework is a key aspect of effective personal judgement.

Professional judgement

Professional judgement, on the other hand, is guided by professional standards, ethical codes and the expectations of the organisation or industry. It involves making decisions that are not only effective but also ethically sound and aligned with the goals of the organisation. Professional judgement often requires a more analytical and structured approach, as it involves complex considerations such as legal compliance, risk management and stakeholder impact.

Despite these differences, effective professional judgement also draws on personal values and ethics. Professionals who can align their personal values with their professional responsibilities are more likely to make decisions that are both ethical and effective. Conversely, conflicts between personal and professional values can lead to ethical dilemmas and impaired judgement. Therefore, the development of EPPJ requires an ongoing process of reflection and alignment between personal and professional identities.

Developing EPPJ: strategies and approaches

Developing EPPJ is a lifelong process that involves continuous learning, reflection and practice. Several strategies can enhance personal and professional judgement, including education, mentorship and experiential learning.

Education and training

Education plays a crucial role in developing the cognitive and ethical foundations of EPPJ. Formal education in fields such as ethics, critical thinking and decision-making provides the theoretical knowledge and analytical skills needed for effective judgement. Professional training programmes, particularly in fields such as law, medicine and business, often include components focused on ethical decision-making and professional judgement.

However, education alone is not sufficient. Effective judgement also requires the ability to apply theoretical knowledge in real-world situations. Therefore, experiential learning – which involves learning through experience and reflection – is an essential component of developing EPPJ.

Mentorship and role models

Mentorship and role models are important influences on the development of EPPJ. Mentors can provide guidance, support and feedback, helping individuals to navigate complex decisions and develop their judgement over time. Role models, particularly those exemplifying strong ethical principles and sound judgement, can inspire and motivate individuals to develop their own judgement.

Mentorship also provides opportunities for reflective practice, where individuals can discuss their experiences, challenges and decisions with a more experienced professional. This reflective process is crucial for developing self-awareness and for refining one's judgement over time.

Reflective practice

Reflective practice involves the systematic examination of one's own experiences and decisions with the aim of learning from them and improving future judgement. This can be done through journaling, discussion with peers or mentors, or formal reflection exercises. Reflective practice encourages individuals to critically evaluate their decisions, to identify areas for improvement and to develop greater self-awareness.

Reflective practice is particularly important in professional settings where decisions often have significant consequences. By reflecting on past decisions, professionals can identify patterns in their judgement, recognise biases and develop strategies for improving their decision-making processes.

Case study

In the United Kingdom, social workers are tasked with delivering services to a diverse population, often encountering individuals with different cultural, socioeconomic and belief systems. The EPPJ model offers a framework for reflective practice, emphasising the need for social workers to critically examine their personal values and beliefs in relation to professional duties. This case study explores the application of the EPPJ model to challenge and reflect on personal biases, improving the quality-of-service delivery and decision-making.

John, a social worker with a local authority, has been working with a family from a different cultural background. The family, originally from a non-European country, holds traditional beliefs regarding gender roles, particularly in parenting and household decision-making. John has noticed that the father appears to have a dominant role in the family, while the mother's contributions seem limited to domestic responsibilities. John, who holds progressive views on gender equality, finds this family dynamic unsettling and begins to feel frustrated with what he perceives as unequal treatment.

As John continues to work with the family, he recognises that his discomfort might stem from his personal values and assumptions about gender roles, which may affect his ability to remain objective in assessing the family's needs. Aware of the risk that his bias could impact his professional judgement, John decides to employ the EPPJ model to reflect on and address his responses to the family's situation.

Reflective exercise

» Under the following headings, consider how John would apply the model to this case.

1. Self-awareness and reflection
2. Critical analysis of personal values
3. Consultation with colleagues and supervision
4. Adjustment of practice

Capture personal reflections and individual thoughts

» Critically reflect on this chapter so far and think about what you have learned. Record your own personal thoughts and feelings.

Chapter summary

EPPJ is a complex and multifaceted concept that draws on cognitive, emotional, ethical and contextual factors. It involves the ability to make sound decisions that are aligned with both personal values and professional standards. The development of EPPJ requires a combination of education, mentorship, reflective practice and experiential learning. As individuals navigate the challenges of personal and professional life, EPPJ serves as a critical tool for making decisions that are not only effective but also ethical and aligned with a broader sense of purpose.

This chapter has provided an overview of EPPJ, exploring its theoretical origins, key influencing factors and strategies for development. Subsequent chapters will delve deeper into specific aspects of EPPJ, examining its application in different professional contexts and exploring the challenges and opportunities that arise in the process of developing and exercising effective judgement. Through a deeper understanding of EPPJ, individuals can enhance their decision-making capabilities, navigate complex ethical dilemmas and achieve greater alignment between their personal and professional lives.

Key takeaways from this chapter

- It is very difficult to detach yourself from your personal values and belief systems when you practise social work.
- The EPPJ model promotes reflection and shows how to use this to combat some of the structural, systemic, community and individual stereotypes and how we act on them.

Chapter 8 | Benefits of EPPJ

Increased personal awareness, increases professional effectiveness.
Arlene P Weekes (2023)

Introduction

This chapter explores the core assertions of the EPPJ framework, emphasising the development of four key skills: awareness, introspection, reflection and self-awareness. The skills are not usually acquired in a linear manner, as they often develop concurrently and are interrelated. However, individuals might acquire them in the following defined order.

1. Self-awareness is *'defined as the human ability to become the object of its own attention, actively identifying, processing, and storing information about the self'* (Majolo et al, 2023).

2. Introspection, *'in contemporary philosophy of mind, is a means of learning about one's own currently ongoing, or perhaps very recently past, mental states or processes. It is the examination of one's own conscious thoughts and feelings'* (Schwitzgebel, 2024).

3. Reflection is *'the process of engaging the self (S) in attentive, critical, exploratory and iterative (ACEI) interactions with one's thoughts and actions (TA), and their underlying conceptual frame (CF), with a view to changing them and a view on the change itself (VC)'* (Nguyen, 2014).

4. *'[A]wareness [is] an understanding of the activities of others, which provides a context for your own activity'* (Dourish and Bellotti, 1992).

By enhancing understanding of one's own values (Reamer, 2013), beliefs and biases, with a focus on personal insight, EPPJ aims to encourage individuals to consider Schön's (1983) concepts of reflection-in-action, reflection-on-action and reflection-for-action, which emphasise the importance of reflecting *in the moment* during an experience, *later/after* the event to analyse its outcomes and *for future action* in preparation for similar situations, thereby enabling practitioners to adapt their actions, enhance learning and improve future practice, given the wider implications for professional decision-making. This self-reflective process ultimately promotes more responsible and informed judgements, aligning personal actions with ethical standards and professional requirements.

Additionally, the chapter highlights the key benefits of the EPPJ framework by comparing EPPJ with other established frameworks and models. The chapter seeks to encourage the reader to engage in a broader discussion and highlights how EPPJ offers a more integrated and holistic approach, combining both emotional and cognitive awareness in decision-making processes by encouraging ongoing reflection and adaptability, thus nurturing an evolving awareness that enhances both personal and professional growth in addressing the complexities of real-world decision-making within social work and other fields.

Three core assertions of EPPJ

Importance of self-awareness in personal and professional contexts

To be effective, individuals need to own their internal and external prejudices. If an individual claims to be non-judgemental, they are denying both internal prejudices and external systematic inequalities, thus denying aspects of themselves and missing an opportunity for real reflection. The responsibility for the management of this lies with both the individual and the professional system in which they operate. The difficulty lies not with the biographical material, but with its individual and organisational containment. Thus, historical material can be experienced as a continuum, from undermining and chaotic to informative and enhancing, providing a tool for challenging what may otherwise be bias, depending on the individual's and the organisation's understanding and management of this material.

The research which gave rise to EPPJ underlines the fact that people are complex, with complex histories and complex views, which they cannot disown, although some attempt to leave them behind when they come to work. In trying to set them aside at work, a sometimes-arid professional stance can result, negating the richness of the experience they could bring to their relational and emotive role. People need to own their individual complexities, because these complexities, consciously or unconsciously, impact on their role and function. In the category of high consciousness and high constructiveness, individuals have a continuous dialogue with themselves about their views and about which experiences are helpful or unhelpful to call upon at which point, so that their experiences impact positively when undertaking tasks. In a state of low consciousness and high constructiveness, as we have noted, individuals leave their complex histories behind in order to remain 'professional' in role. Those individuals with low consciousness and low constructiveness carry the burden of their complex lives around with them and it appears to drive much of what they do. This can be useful in challenging tired narratives and professional distancing, but is often experienced negatively, as they rarely demonstrate a reflective dialogue with themselves, raising the question of how a person can be a useful panel member if they are dislocated from or ruled by their personal biography.

Examples of complex experiences

In the 1990s, Vincent Felitti et al (1998) referred to potentially traumatic events including abuse, neglect and household dysfunction. This was expanded by Young Minds (2018), which described Adverse Childhood Experiences (ACEs) as

highly stressful, and potentially traumatic, events or situations that occur during childhood and/or adolescence [occurring before age 18]. They can be a single event, or prolonged threats to, and breaches of, the young person's safety, security, trust or bodily integrity.

Similarly, Post-Traumatic Stress Disorder (PTSD), documented by Hippocrates (4607–377 BC) and Jean-Martin Charcot (1825–93) and conceptualised by psychiatrists after observing soldiers in combat, following World Wars I and II (including Holocaust survivors), Vietnam veterans and rape and domestic abuse survivors, is a mental health condition triggered by traumatic events, leading to symptoms such as flashbacks, distorted memory and emotional responses, severe anxiety and emotional numbness. The concept of the narrative identity, explored by Dan McAdams (1993), refers to the internalised and evolving story individuals create about themselves, encompassing their experiences, beliefs and values, which shapes their sense of self and guides their behaviour. The negative experiences of trauma can lead to a distorted self-concept that has entrenched feelings of victimisation, helplessness and inadequacy, and struggles that hinder emotional well-being, personal growth and development.

As mentioned in Chapter 4 on the wounded healer, while challenges exist, understanding one's lived experiences – especially those shaped by adversity – can greatly enhance personal and professional growth. Reflecting on these experiences can boosts self-awareness, revealing how past events influence current behaviours, emotions and decisions, and potentially promote emotional resilience if one's narrative identity is reframed. By examining aspects such as ACEs and PTSD, individuals can recognise how these histories shape their interactions and emotional responses. The idea of emotional intelligence (EI), also known as Emotional Quotient (EQ), was developed by Salovey and Mayer (1990) and popularised by Daniel Goleman (1995); it further enhances these processes, allowing individuals to manage their emotions and recognise their impact on thoughts and behaviours. Additionally, shadow work, derived from Jung's (1961, 1962) concept, encourages exploration of repressed feelings and traits, leading to a more authentic self.

Ultimately, an individual's journey not only has the potential to improve their personal well-being; it also equips them to support others effectively, turning their healing into a source of strength and insight.

Prejudging: the idea that being non-judgemental is a fallacy

It astounds the authors that professions that assess risk, strengths and resources continue to promote and teach students and practitioners to be non-judgemental. Instead, these professions should encourage the examination biases to their students, and make it clear that non-discrimination, anti-oppression and anti-racism are taught and promoted.

The fundamental idea behind EPPJ is that the notion of being non-judgemental is a fallacy. The aim then becomes supporting, empowering and educating people to be consciously aware of their inherent personal and professional judgements so they can be significantly more effective in undertaking their role and function. By recognising, analysing and adapting personal values and beliefs, decision-makers could enhance their professionalism, particularly in relation to decisions about others. This is where EPPJ can be most usefully deployed.

Judging people based on preconceived ideas is extremely common in everyday life. Sometimes these judgements are very subtle and can even be well-meaning. Often, they are called 'microaggressions'. A recruitment manager, for example, may draw conclusions about applicants based on their own personal beliefs, then look for behaviours during the interview process that 'confirm' those biases. Or take the frequently occurring example where someone from the global majority is asked where they are from, then questioned in detail about their parents' heritage if the initial answer is that they are British. It may be well-intentioned, but it is still a microaggression, resulting from a place of bias.

Or consider the situation where a woman is walking alone at night and hears footsteps running behind her. She has several courses of action open to her. She can slow down to allow the person running behind her to pass, or she can consider being self-defensive should she be attacked or call a friend on her mobile as she walks. She could scream to alert passers-by that the man 'is a rapist' (which in this case he isn't). If she does this, not knowing who the person is, it is arguably a form of discrimination; she is acting on preconceived ideas and as a result prejudging and discriminating against another person. Prejudging the situation in order to keep herself safe isn't the problem; the problem is acting on her prejudgements – for example by calling the man a rapist.

In group situations, discussions can sometimes become unfocused, resulting in a failure to address and resolve key issues. This is especially common in complex situations, where the dynamics of group interaction may lead to unconscious value judgements rather than objective, evidence-based decision-making.

Below is an example of an interchange between panel members that illustrates this. It is based on an actual case, although it has been slightly edited for clarity and confidentiality. A local authority fostering panel was discussing the case of a foster carer whose marriage had broken down and who was now separated. The continued suitability of the female foster carer was now in question. Rather than querying suitability, the panel became diverted by the issue of in-care planning for the child, rather than attempting to establish whether the carer remained suitable. Note how the following exchange is more of a value-based dialogue consisting of statements (not questions), rather than an examination of the evidence, and how value judgements were made by several panel members, including the chair.

The exchange

Chair
: *I mean ... I don't want to pass comment or judgement now, but I need to say that I find it unusual that L appears not to have had any contact with B and the family. Because if they have income, like the renting for example, what is happening to that income? And given that he was not working before, how is he surviving now financially?*

    Is B receiving any income from the rented house? You see what I mean? I just find it unusual that, you know ... that she's saying she doesn't really know much about his whereabouts. Without wanting to, you know, say that she's not being truthful.

Panel member
: *I don't ... from my knowledge of relationships, people don't usually just wake up one day and walk out. Well, they probably do, I don't know. But there's more to it than that. But we need to focus on the children. And how is she coping with the whole thing? Because there's the children's needs, and there's what she needs to do her job well. And, if those things are not dealt with ...*

Chair
: *That's why it's important that L should, you know, show some responsibility for them, at least in terms of the letter, he owes that to the children and also the Local Authority, because he was approved as a carer. So, it's not a big ask, I think, for him to provide some closure to the children in terms of an explanation. Then they can also, you know, be less worried and understand and continue their lives with you, because clearly, they're worried about you. They shouldn't be, but they are.*

    I think those letters must continue and I think that he must have a discussion with a social worker, preferably you. He needs to provide an explanation to each child. Because he's doing that with M, he's talking with him, but he's not talking with the other three children.

Becoming a reflective practitioner

Although there are numerous models, frameworks and resources available that may assist practitioners and students to become more reflective, research (Finlay, 2008; Middleton, 2017; Platt, 2014) points to the challenges of developing into and maintaining the ability of being a reflective practitioner over time. Our own experience of attempting to support students to become reflective practitioners attests to their findings. Dr Weekes recalls the moans, despair and hopelessness that many of the students had when they were unable to achieve the demonstration in their weekly formative written assignment. Two weeks before the semester or class ended, I invited every student in the class to physically answer one of three questions: who 'got' reflection the first time? Who eventually became proficient at it? Who still had not mastered it? No one in the MA class, but one student in the BA class, stood up in response to the first question. The majority of the class stood up in answer to the second question for both groups. About 15–25 per cent of the students in both classes were standing to signify that they had failed to demonstrate the ability to articulate the skill of reflection in any of their prior attempts to write a weekly 500-word reflection with two weeks left in the course. This experience is shared to first reinforce the work of Finlay (2008), Platt (2014) and Middleton (2017), but also to draw the reader's attention to the fact that being a reflective practitioner is not a straightforward skill for individuals in general to acquire, and for some it may never be mastered.

This is raised because professionals are increasingly expected to be solution-focused in many fields and areas of life – but *whose* solution is chosen and why? Each of us has a modus operandi, namely a particular approach to or method of executing matters, commonly characterising a person's routines, habits or usual approach to tasks or problems. By this point in the book, it should be clear to the reader that EPPJ as a framework would assert that the chosen method depends on our individual experiences, values and belief system. This means the different models or frameworks are summarised so the reader is likely to have a leaning towards one or the other. However, rather than justifying why one model is preferred, you are encouraged to embrace the benefits of EPPJ. Unlike a step-by-step model that claims to lead to reflection, EPPJ is a framework of self-discovery. It acknowledges that you never fully arrive at complete understanding, as there is always more to learn about yourself.

The comparison of EPPJ with other models and frameworks

So as not to inadvertently show a preference, the models are listed in chronological order of their known conception.

Borton's framework

Borton's (1970) framework revolves around the questions 'What?', 'So what?' and 'Now what?' (Figure 8.1). Self-awareness is developed as practitioners think about the consequences of their actions while working on the four skills. The investigation of individual motivations promotes introspection.

By including structured questions like 'What did I learn?' and 'What will I do differently next time?', Driscoll (2007) extended Borton's 1970 framework, encouraging the practical application of reflection without delving deeper into ethical issues. This was further expanded upon by Rolfe et al (2001), who encouraged a more critical study by relating comments to theory and posing the question of why events occurred. Nevertheless, neither framework incorporates the ethical reflection and focus on self-knowledge and awareness that EPPJ does, which makes EPPJ better suited for morally challenging work settings.

Note that there are other similar reflective processes that add additional questions: who? What? When? Where? Why? Which? And How?

Kolb's learning model

Kolb (1984) emphasises the cyclical process of learning from experience, urging individuals to participate in active experimentation, abstract conceptualisation, reflective observation and concrete experience (Figure 8.2). This model is well known for its

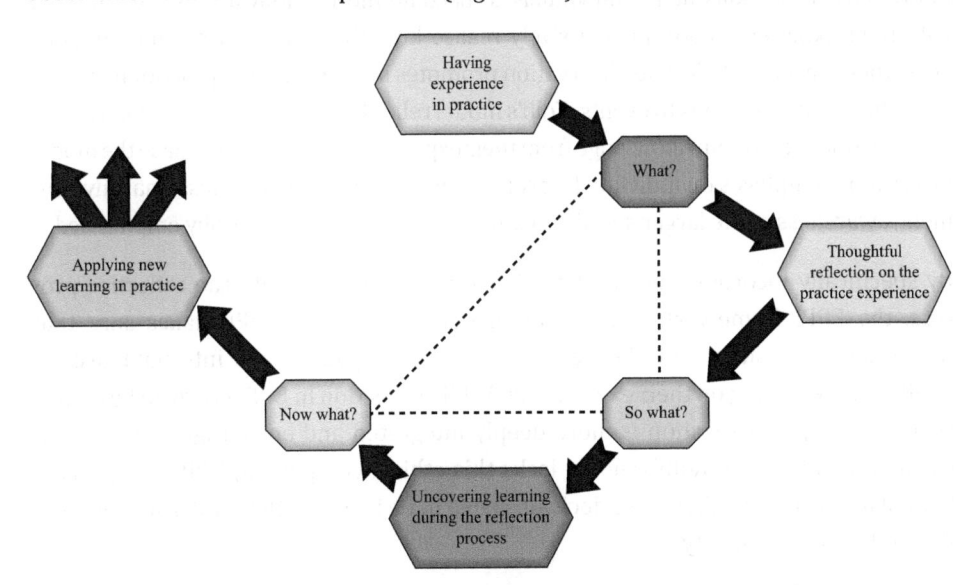

Figure 8.1 Adaption and combining of Borton's (1970) framework developed by Driscoll (1994) and Rolfe et al (2001)

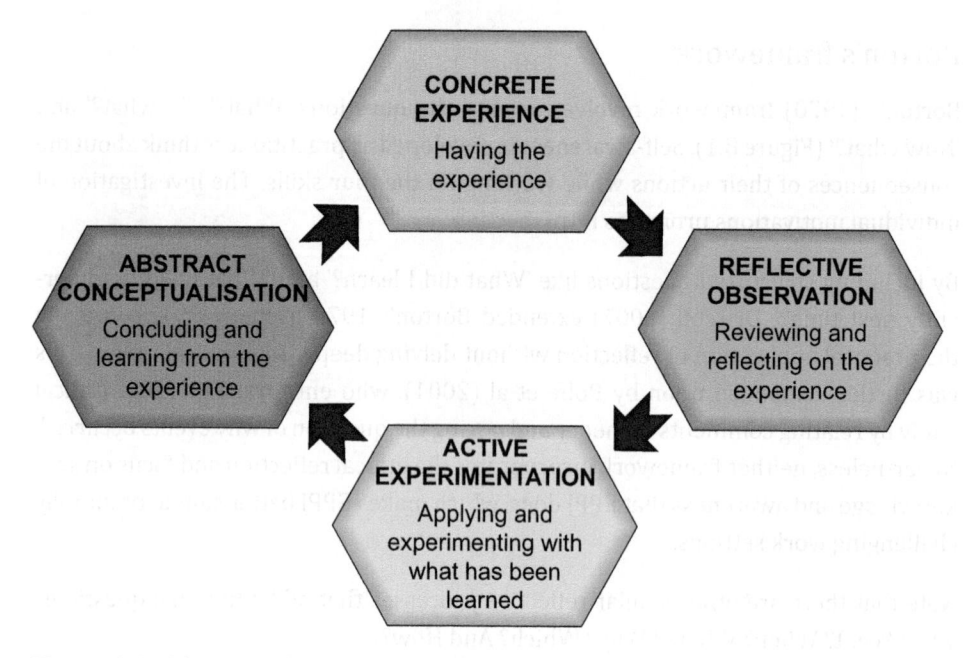

Figure 8.2 Adaption of Kolb's (1984) experiential learning model

methodical approach to experiential learning, which makes it an effective instrument for both education and professional development.

Addressing these skills helps individuals to become more self-aware as they interact with their experiences and progressively realise how their own biases and emotions affect their learning. Reflective observation promotes introspection as practitioners consider their inner reactions to events. Kolb's model relies heavily on reflection, which enables practitioners to gain knowledge from their experiences. However, because the model places more emphasis on individual learning than on the external professional environment, awareness of the larger social and ethical context is not specifically emphasised.

By specifically incorporating self-knowledge and awareness into the reflective process, the EPPJ framework expands upon Kolb's approach. EPPJ makes sure that practitioners consider both their external ethical obligations and internal biases in addition to reflecting on their experiences. While reflection in EPPJ is driven by ethical requirements, introspection is more deeply integrated and encourages critical self-examination. Because Kolb's model lacks this ethical component, EPPJ is especially helpful for professionals, whose decisions need to be in line with moral principles and their influence on society.

The reflective process

By encouraging individuals to critically examine their experiences and extract lessons for future practice, the model places a strong emphasis on the concept of learning from experience through reflection (Figure 8.3), which adds a recognised contribution to professional development.

```
┌─────────────┐      ┌──────────────────────────┐      ┌──────────────────────────┐
│ Experience  │      │    Reflective process    │      │        Outcomes          │
│ Behaviour   │ ───▶ │ Returning to the experience│ ───▶ │ New perspectives on      │
│ Ideas       │ ◀─── │ Attending to feelings    │      │ experiences              │
│ Feelings    │      │ Re-evaluting the experience│     │ Change in behaviour      │
│             │      │                          │      │ Readiness for application│
│             │      │                          │      │ Commitment to action     │
└─────────────┘      └──────────────────────────┘      └──────────────────────────┘
```

Figure 8.3 Boud et al's (1985) model of reflection or 'the reflective process'

Examining one's own experiences helps develop self-awareness when working on the four skills. As practitioners evaluate their feelings and thoughts in relation to these experiences, introspection is encouraged. The model also stresses a comprehension of learning objectives and context awareness.

By including ethical considerations into the reflective process, EPPJ enhances this model, ensuring that reflections not only promote personal growth but also lead to responsible and morally sound professional actions. This ethical dimension makes EPPJ particularly valuable for practitioners in fields with significant ethical responsibilities.

Brookfield's reflective model (1988)

The significance of critically analysing one's own presumptions and beliefs in professional activity is emphasised by Brookfield's (1988) model (Figure 8.4). Challenging individuals to engage in critical reflection, this model encourages a multifaceted approach through four distinct lenses: the *self-reflection lens*, which encourages introspection on personal experiences and responses; the *user lens*, which considers input from those impacted by one's work, aimed at encouraging empathy and understanding; the *colleagues' insights lens*, which gathers insight from peers; and the *theoretical and organisational lens*, integrating relevant literature, professional and organisational perspectives and knowledge to enhance professional practice to support informed decision-making.

```
┌─────────────┐      ┌─────────────┐
│    SELF-    │ ───▶ │   USER'S    │
│  REFLECTION │      │  VIEWPOINT  │
└─────────────┘      └─────────────┘
      ▲                     │
      │                     ▼
┌─────────────┐      ┌─────────────┐
│             │      │ THEORETICAL │
│ COLLEAGUES' │ ◀─── │     AND     │
│   INSIGHTS  │      │ORGANISATIONAL│
│             │      │ PERSPECTIVES│
└─────────────┘      └─────────────┘
```

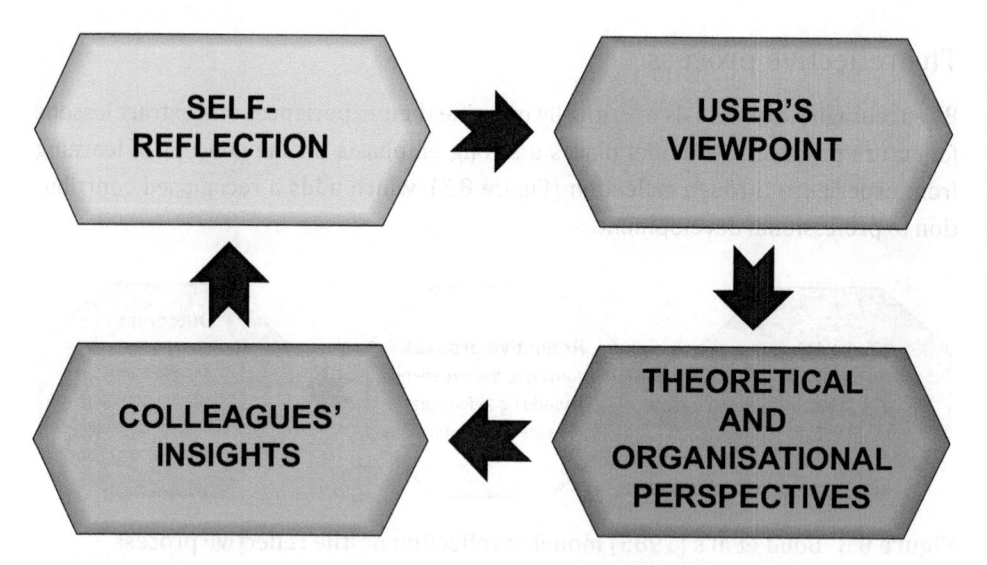

Figure 8.4 Adaption of Brookfield's (1988) reflective model

As individuals are encouraged to face their underlying beliefs, Brookfield's (1988) model centres on comprehending one's own presumptions without a clear ethical component, in terms of the four skills. Critical analysis of one's own experiences encourages introspection, whereas a variety of perspectives promotes contemplation. On the other hand, EPPJ incorporates ethical considerations straight into the reflective process in addition to promoting profound self-awareness and introspection. EPPJ is especially pertinent in disciplines that need ethical decision-making since it guarantees that practitioners not only acknowledge their presumptions but also evaluate their moral consequences in professional circumstances.

Gibbs' reflective cycle (1988)

As a simple, methodical, systematic, experience-based learning approach, Gibbs' (1988) reflective cycle encourages individuals to explain their experiences, leading individuals through the stages of reflection, from description to action planning, by examining their emotions, assessing their results and making inferences for future work (Figure 8.5). Examining one's own emotions in relation to experiences promotes self-awareness when working on the four skills. As individuals examine their emotional reactions, introspection takes place, practised in a plain and approachable manner. While knowledge of the consequences of their actions is emphasised, the cycle's planned steps promote reflection.

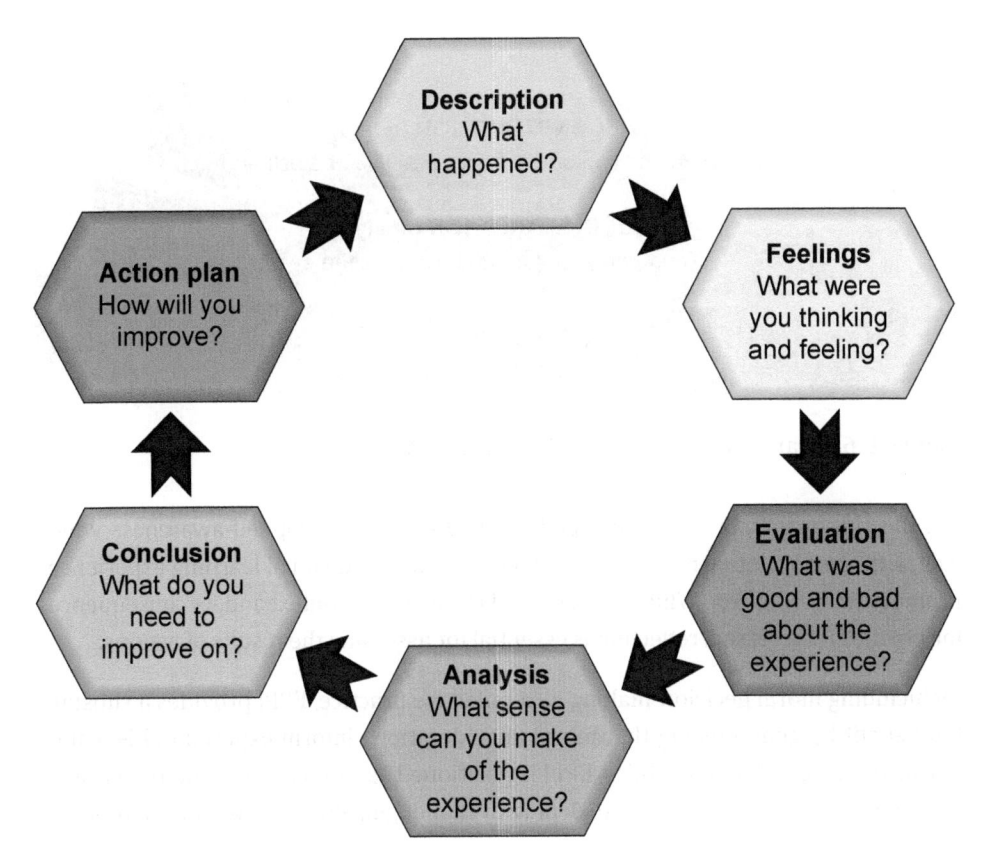

Figure 8.5 Gibbs' (1988) reflective cycle

By adding ethical considerations into each reflective step, EPPJ offers an alternative to Gibbs' (1988) model by making sure that reflections address both the moral implications of actions made and personal insights. EPPJ stands out as a more thorough framework for professional practice because of its emphasis on moral judgement, resulting in decisions that are ethically informed.

Fook's inductive process (2002)

With an emphasis on critical reflective practice, Fook's (2002) inductive process promotes experiential learning as a way to build professional competences, via the stages of telling the narrative, deconstructing and reconstructing the situation (Figure 8.6). The model encourages individuals to take lessons from their past experiences and modify their practice accordingly.

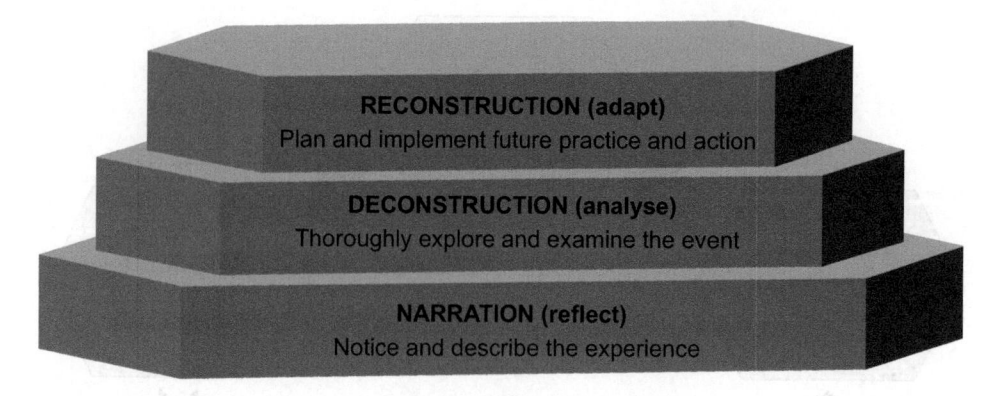

RECONSTRUCTION (adapt)
Plan and implement future practice and action

DECONSTRUCTION (analyse)
Thoroughly explore and examine the event

NARRATION (reflect)
Notice and describe the experience

Figure 8.6 Adaption of Fook's (2002) inductive process

By reflecting on their prejudices and beliefs, practitioners develop self-awareness, which aids with the development of the four skills. Analysing individual learning experiences promotes introspection. While awareness of the learning context and its consequences for practice is increased, reflection is essential for assessing the results of actions.

By including moral decision-making into reflective practice, EPPJ provides a substantial benefit by guaranteeing that moral considerations inform experiential learning. Because of its emphasis on ethics, EPPJ is positioned as a more comprehensive framework for practitioners who have to deal with challenging ethical situations in practice.

Korthagen and Vasalos's onion model (2005)

This cyclical 'onion' approach to reflection (Korthagen and Vasalos, 2005) stresses that an individual level of reflection is dependent upon how deep they wish to go, namely do they wish to peel off the layers (Figure 8.7). It involves asking different and deeper questions as each layer is peeled back. What action is taken, what is observed and what is assessed will determine the promotion of both professional and personal development. This paradigm emphasises how experience and reflection are intertwined, which promotes continuous learning and practice modification.

As individuals assess their own behaviours and reactions, the model supports the acquisition of the four skills. Analysing the feelings and motivations associated with events encourages introspection. Since the cyclical nature promotes ongoing improvement, reflection is essential. Understanding the social context of one's professional behaviour improves awareness.

By including ethical decision-making into the reflective cycle and guaranteeing that reflections result in responsible actions, EPPJ is an enhancement to this model. This clear emphasis on ethical considerations enables individuals to align their professional

Environment
(What do you have to deal with?)

Behaviour
(What do you do?)

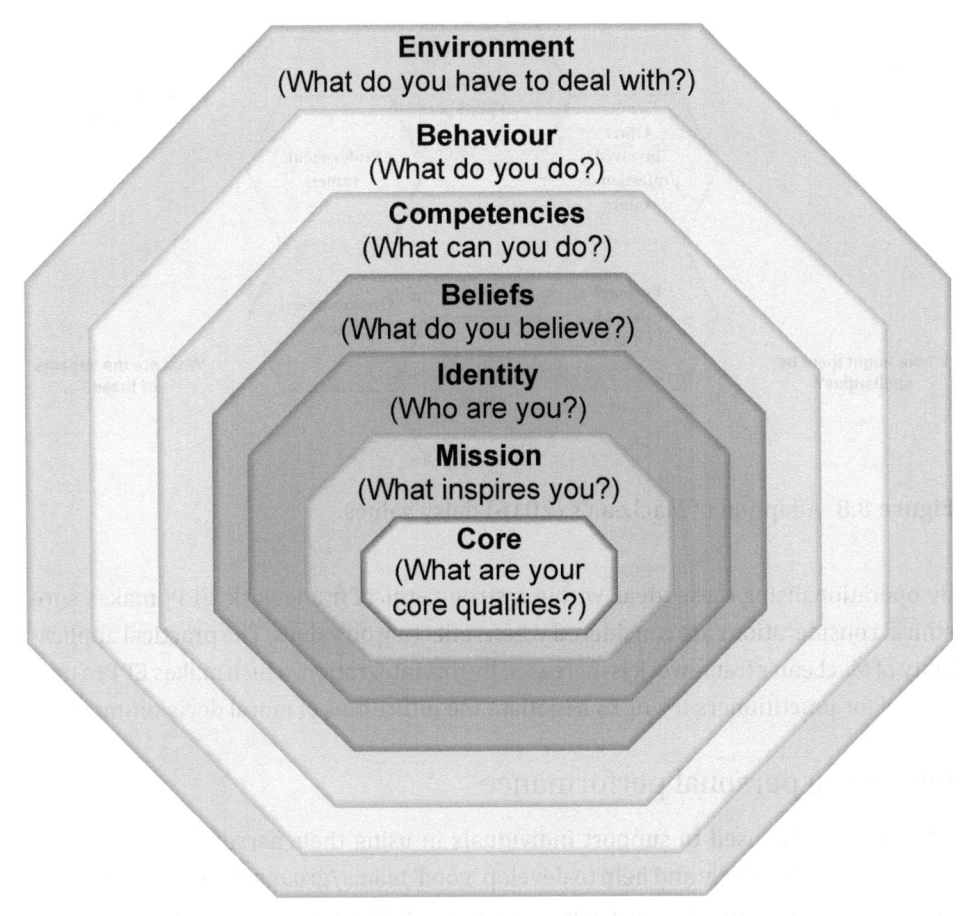

Competencies
(What can you do?)

Beliefs
(What do you believe?)

Identity
(Who are you?)

Mission
(What inspires you?)

Core
(What are your core qualities?)

Figure 8.7 Adaption of Korthagen and Vasalos's (2005) onion model

responsibilities with their personal insights, promoting both professional development and moral integrity.

Daisy values by MacLean (2016)

MacLean's (2016) daisy values model highlights how crucial it is to identify and express one's own values in one's professional life (Figure 8.8). The purpose of this approach is to encourage critical thinking about how values influence choices.

Self-awareness is essential to the four skills since it allows practitioners to recognise their basic beliefs. Thinking on how these values affect behaviour promotes introspection.

While awareness of the relevance of values in decision-making is stressed, reflection is about assessing how well values match with professional practice.

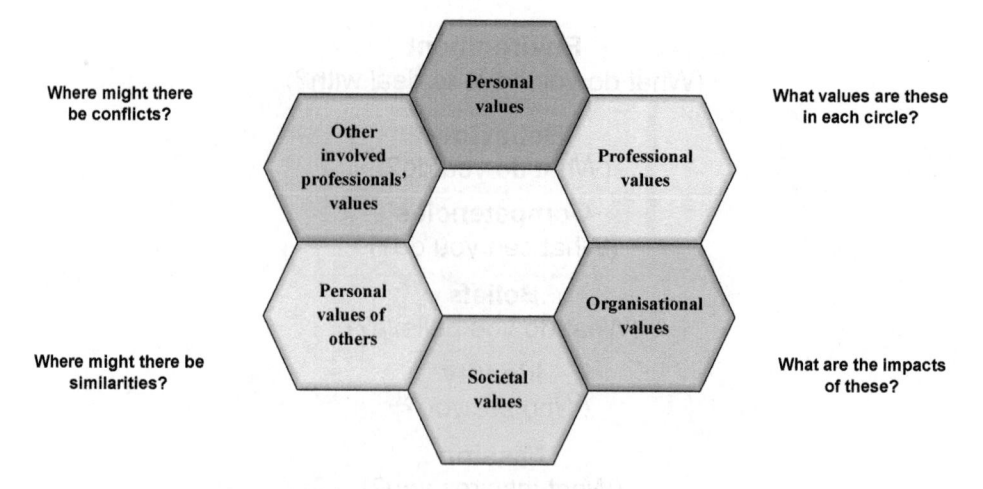

Figure 8.8 Adaption of MacLean's (2016) daisy values

By operationalising these ideas within a strong ethical framework, EPPJ makes sure ethical considerations are considered when reflecting on values. The practical applicability of MacLean's framework is increased by this integration, which makes EPPJ a useful tool for practitioners trying to negotiate the difficulties of moral decision-making.

Improving personal performance

EPPJ can also be used to support individuals in using their personal biography, so they function effectively and help to develop 'good' teams/groups. In contrast, a team/group may benefit from having some members from the low consciousness/high constructiveness quadrant, as research shows that some individuals, while essentially guarded about the information they share, demonstrate an ability to remain on task. It is clear from contrasting various frameworks and models with the EPPJ framework that the latter provides a distinct benefit by integrating moral judgement into the reflective process. This unique integration promotes professional integrity and efficacy in challenging ethical environments by enabling practitioners to consider their experiences and ideals as well as ensure that their actions are in line with their moral obligations. Based on their applicability and contributions to the subject of sound personal and professional judgement, you might choose particular models from this overview to emphasise in your practice.

Improving effectiveness in work situations

EPPJ can, for example, be used when considering team recruitment and membership, ensuring teams are limited to one or two individuals in the low consciousness/low constructiveness quadrant, while recognising that teams and groups may benefit from these individuals to produce a challenge to those in the reflective and professional quadrants. Such a challenge would help the individuals concerned develop some personal and professional distance from their internal drivers. Such people need to cultivate the capacity to self-manage and be assisted by the panel chair to self-regulate.

In short, EPPJ is an important first step in helping people to be more aware of their own biographies and the effect of those biographies on their work, and in particular their decision-making. By using EPPJ, decisions will be fairer and more objective, and help to deliver better life outcomes for children in the public care system.

Reflective exercise

Comparing the EPPJ framework with other models

Objective: This exercise encourages deeper engagement and understanding of both the EPPJ Framework and the selected models, identifying similarities, differences and implications. It aims to encourage critical thinking, self-awareness and practical application in real-world contexts.

Duration: Allow at least one hour for this exercise.

Format: Choose to write your reflections in a journal, create a mind map or discuss your thoughts with a peer or mentor for additional perspectives.

Steps

1. Select a model
   » Choose one of the eight framework or models referred to in the chapter and do the following.
2. Read and reflect
   » Review the EPPJ Framework
   » Review the selected model
3. Comparative analysis and reflection – in a reflective journal, write a response to the following prompts.
   » Similarities: identify and discuss at least three similarities between the EPPJ Framework and the chosen model. Consider aspects such as:

- how both frameworks promote self-reflection;
- the emphasis on personal and professional growth;
- the role of awareness (emotional, self or values).

» *Differences*: Identify and discuss at least three differences between the EPPJ Framework and the chosen model. Reflect on:
- the focus of each model (eg practical judgement vs emotional intelligence);
- the structure or format of the models (eg visual representation vs conceptual framework);
- the contexts in which each model may be most effective.

» *Implications*: Discuss and summarise the implications of using the EPPJ Framework rather than your chosen model. Highlight the key takeaways from your comparative analysis. Consider how this exercise has influenced your understanding of EPPJ and its importance in your personal and professional contexts and could inform your future decision-making or reflective practices.

Chapter summary

This chapter has highlighted that EPPJ represents a continuous journey, which is essential for personal growth and professional development. EPPJ encourages the development of four core skills: awareness, introspection, reflection and self-awareness, all of which assist an individual to become a reflective practitioner, prompting individuals to consciously recognise their judgements and understand how their social, cultural and professional contexts shape these decisions. Reflecting on one's position (Weekes, 2023) within power structures enables individuals to comprehend and address their inherent biases, resulting in increased work effectiveness and heightened personal awareness.

The chapter contrasts EPPJ with other frameworks and models that generally emphasise rigid, systematic approaches, and do not focus on ethical decision-making. In contrast to these models, EPPJ promotes a comprehensive and flexible perspective, facilitating the incorporation of emotional intelligence and empathy in evaluative processes. This framework produces multiple advantages, such as enhanced decision-making, improved relationships and greater resilience in professional settings.

Thus, decisions – or choosing between options about 'best' outcomes – should be based on EPPJ. By recognising, analysing and adapting personal values and preferences, decision-makers will become professionally proficient, particularly in relation to decisions about others. This concept could have a wide impact. It could, for example, be used when considering team membership, ensuring that teams have no more than one or two individuals in the low consciousness/low constructiveness quadrant, while recognising that teams and groups may benefit from these individuals to produce a challenge to those in the reflective and professional quadrants, in order that the latter can develop some personal and professional distance from their internal drivers. Such people need to cultivate the capacity to self-manage and be helped to self-regulate by the meeting chair/their managers. In 'good' meetings and teams, if they are 'held', they can be supported to use their personal biography to function effectively. In contrast, a team or panel may benefit from having some members from the low consciousness and high constructiveness quadrant; data analysis in the original research found some panel members who, while guarded about what they shared, demonstrated an ability to remain on task. Such people need to be encouraged to be more empathetic, by the appropriate sharing of their experiences and selves, and to develop a less officious manner. This highlights the significance of continuous reflection and self-assessment, incorporating EPPJ into leadership and team dynamics to cultivate a culture of reflective practice that alters professional roles and improves organisational effectiveness.

Key takeaways from this chapter

- EPPJ outlines broader principles and is used to support thinking rather than being a specific technique or practice. It is more accurately described as a framework designed to guide effective judgement and reflection in personal and professional contexts.

- EPPJ provides a structured *framework* of thinking about or approaching complex issues, enabling individuals to reflect on and make sound judgements that balance both personal and professional aspects of their lives.

- EPPJ embodies elements of a *conceptual idea* revolving around integrating personal and professional judgement – its real strength lies in its application as a framework for action and reflection.

Chapter 9 | Identifying your category: the EPPJ web tool

What Is It That I Search 4 ... what it is that I search 4.
Tupac Shakur (1999)

Introduction

In the realm of decision-making, understanding your personal and professional judgements is crucial. The framework, which was developed following Dr Weekes' (2020) insightful PhD research, is used to guide you through the process of identifying your EPPJ category in this chapter. The instrument was meticulously designed in collaboration with a psychologist following this research, incorporating feedback from over 300 individuals during the testing phase. This meticulous process guarantees that the EPPJ tool is both valid and dependable, thereby increasing its efficacy for users.

Understanding your EPPJ category is not just about knowing where you stand; it is about harnessing that knowledge to make more balanced and objective decisions. This chapter highlights the four main categories and six sub-categories of the EPPJ framework, offering a glimpse into how each category affects your judgements and decision-making. In addition, it provides testimonials from individuals who have personally encountered the transformative power of this tool, as well as the potential pitfalls of attempting to determine their category without using it.

The chapter concludes by encouraging you to embark on this journey of self-discovery and uncover the potential for more effective decision-making in your life. The initial phase is straightforward: simply head to www.eppj.org to begin this assessment.

The research

Chapter 1 offered convincing evidence that providing individuals with a means of understanding their consciousness/constructiveness profile benefits them professionally in several ways. As a result, the entire panel system, at a holistic level, also benefits. The research showed the following.

» Individuals who are aware of their own biographies are better able to make more dispassionate professional recommendations and decisions.

» Such individuals are also significantly more effective in understanding and executing their role and function.

» By recognising, analysing and adapting personal values and preferences, decision-makers will become professionally proficient, particularly in relation to decisions about others.

» Panels that consist of individuals with a mix of consciousness/constructiveness profiles can function more effectively. For example, a team or panel may benefit from having some members from the low consciousness/high constructiveness quadrant.

Constructiveness
Self-awareness of personal attitudes, beliefs and values

Consciousness
Use of biography in performing role / task

Individuals who are self-aware but do not put that knowledge into practice. These individuals could be trained to use their experiences more effectively.	Individuals are sufficiently aware of themselves to make an effective contribution as an individual. These individuals know what they are doing and tend to do it.
Individuals have pockets of self-knowledge but do not use the knowledge effectively. These individuals have unregulated emotional states and thought patterns that can impair their effectiveness.	Individuals do not demonstrate high self-awareness but have professional competence to be effective in role. These individuals can be supported and trained to bring their self to the task.

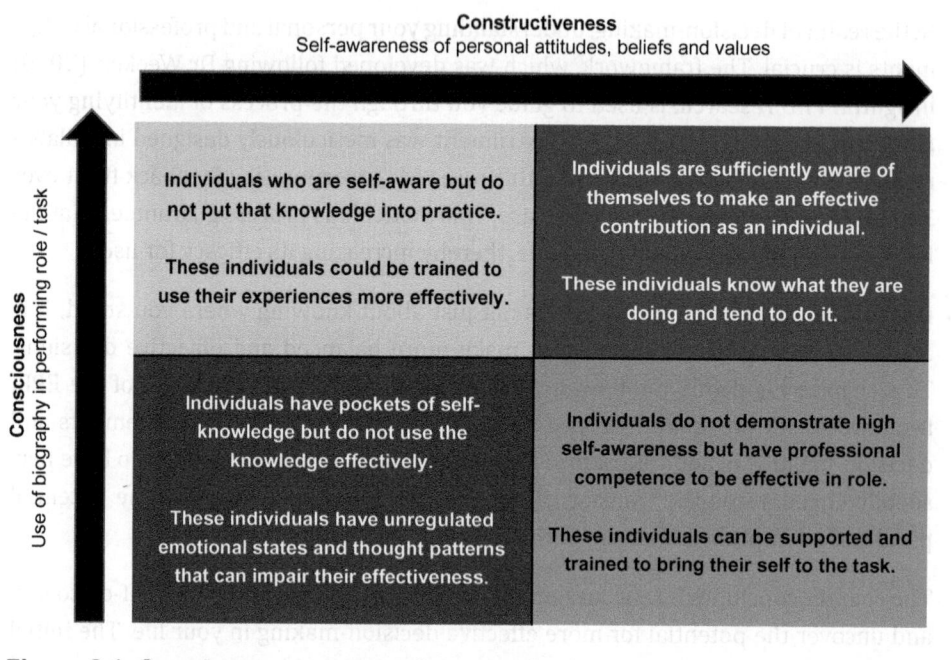

Figure 9.1 Consciousness–constructiveness axle

The four categories of decision-making are defined in Figure 9.1 above as follows.

1. Individuals with *high consciousness and low constructiveness* are characterised as self-aware but choose not to use their awareness constructively.

2. Those with *high consciousness and high constructiveness* possess awareness of both themselves and external factors, leading to more constructive decisions.

3. Individuals characterised by *low consciousness and low constructiveness* are generally unaware of their internal influences, resulting in unconstructive decision-making.
4. Those with *low consciousness and high constructiveness* may lack self-awareness, yet appear competent in decision-making, often coming across as mechanical and detached.

The first step in applying EPPJ

The first step is the identification of which consciousness/constructiveness category best describes you. To assist the reader, a web-based tool was devised that is quick and easy to use. All you need to do is complete the questionnaire (56 questions, based on a five-point Likert scale (see Figure 9.2).

	Please indicate which statement describes you best					
		Strongly disagree	Disagree	Neutral	Agree	Strongly agree
5	I can see the impact of education and experiences related to it on my life.	1	2	3	4	5
12	My relationships with my relatives have been mostly positive.	1	2	3	4	5
24	No matter the cost, I will do what it takes to get the job done.	1	2	3	4	5
31	Sometimes I take action before listening completely to my colleagues.	5	4	3	2	1
49	I seek recognition within my community.	5	4	3	2	1
6	I avoid conflicts or dealing with conflicts or confrontational situations.					

Figure 9.2 By completing the EPPJ questionnaire, you will learn which main category (see Chapter 5) describes you best

The tool will automatically assess your responses and tell you which category you fall into (see Figure 9.2). You will be scored against the sub-categories (see Figure 9.3).

Table 9.1 The EPPJ questionnaire also indicates your level of consciousness/constructiveness in each of six sub-categories

Self Score: >33	Self Score: <33
Individuals with higher levels of self-awareness have a better understanding of how they affect the environment and those around them. They are also ...	Individuals with low self-awareness are often characterised by a lack of critical thinking, about themselves and others. They have ...
Family Score: >30	Family Score: <30
Individuals in this sub-category are likely to have high self-esteem and self-confidence. Able to be ...	People in this sub-category may have had their individuality suppressed during formative years, which can lead to ...
Occupation Score: >75	Occupation Score: <75
People like yourself, with a positive job/career history often have high levels of autonomy and a good ability to focus on a task. They ...	Those in this sub-category often lack independent drive and are sometimes too ready to ...

It also tells you how six other important aspects of your background and character can affect your decision-making. These six aspects, or six sub-categories, influencing personal and professional judgements include: *sense of self*, which involves self-awareness and understanding of values, beliefs and biases; *family history*, which examines how upbringing and relationships shape worldviews and judgements; *professional background*, highlighting how experiences and education contribute to decision-making skills; *professional presentation*, focusing on communication style and appearance, which affect credibility and trust; *sense of community*, referring to connections within social networks that enhance collaborative decision-making; and *sense of group belonging*, which explores identification with teams that fosters loyalty and enhances teamwork. Together, these sub-categories form a framework for understanding and improving judgement in various contexts.

Together, the categories and sub-categories provide a comprehensive framework for understanding how personal and professional judgements are shaped, promoting growth and adaptability in various contexts.

What this means in practice

When you know your consciousness/constructiveness 'profile', you will be more aware of how your temperament and biases affect your judgement and can take action to use your background more constructively in the decision-making process. This is supported by the results of several studies, particularly the research by Dr Weekes (2000) upon which EPPJ is based.

The voices of those who have used the tool

The following quotes are from practitioners/social workers and managers who used the tool. You will notice that they range across the axis.

The yellow corner

The questions themselves were easy, and I initially did not think that from the questions that were asked you would be able to determine how any personal values, beliefs and prejudices influence the decisions I made. After fully reading the report, I could not believe how accurate it was to how I am as a person. For example it states, 'People in this category ... may see them as lacking empathy for those faced with problems as they feel they are dealing with issues fairly and realistically'. This is something that regularly comes up in conversation in my personal life, whereby because I look at the problem and try to fix it people do not think I have any empathy, when I do but my way of showing that is trying to deal with the issues at hand. I enjoyed being able to have the opportunity to try the questionnaire out and am affirmed by the results. It's so weird to have myself written about so accurately just by answering what you perceive to be a simple set of questions.

LC

The blue dimension

It was good to kind of confirm how my life experiences have shaped my thought. I know I have made conscious effort regardless of my circumstances to be aware of who I am personally and professionally. I have noticed things such as how my need for recognition can sometimes be self-serving and have to often ensure to combat that I also give others recognition. I have been saying a lot lately that I am desensitised due to my life experiences but the message about sometimes lacking empathy which was in the professional presentation section really made sense to me.

AJ

The green zone

I'm probably now a lot more conscious of the impact that history has had on me ... That that confidence comes from the fact that I understand what the tools are trying to achieve and I understand who I am right. Or at least, ironically, I understand that I don't understand who I am.

Well, maybe what I'm proving is that people in that box are exactly the people that are gonna struggle to use the tool because they're people that struggle to use their childhood. I'm in that green box because I struggled to apply my history.

Yeah, and the things I know about myself from childhood, I struggle or I should know about myself. I struggle to apply those to work. Yeah.

But surely that also puts me in the category of people who would struggle to take meaning from this tool and then apply it because I'm already bad at doing that process.

SG

Red sphere

I believe this characterisation somewhat resonates with me in my current stage of life and the EPPJ approach enables a chance for me to self-reflect on this to ensure I make sound judgements.

Anonymous

Reflective exercise

» Complete the EPPJ tool at www.eppj.org for a full personal analysis. Completing the questionnaire takes less than 15 minutes, and within moments of submission you will receive a detailed report highlighting your position on the consciousness–constructiveness axis and its implications across six key areas: self, family, professional presentation, occupation, community and group.

» Using the information, complete the section of the report that provides spaces for users to reflect on their category and sub-category results. It includes prompts to help users consider how they will apply this information in their decision-making process.

» Complete the reflective questions at the end of your report once you have completed the tool.

Chapter summary

This chapter has examined the EPPJ framework, which was developed following Dr Weekes' (2000) PhD social work research on the biographic and professional influences of decision-making and attitudes, and designed with a psychologist to assist individuals in identifying their EPPJ category – which is critical for effective engagement in decision-making processes. Drawing from the research, the chapter outlined the development of the tool, which comprises four primary categories and six sub-categories. The framework emphasises the importance of self-awareness, illustrating that understanding one's personal biases and influences can lead to better decisions. Through practical scoring methods and positive testimonials, Dr Weekes highlights how increased personal awareness increases professional effectiveness.

EPPJ recognises that everyone is who they are – the experiences that shape an individual occur for a reason. An individual is who they are, and who they are is who they are meant to be. It isn't about comparing oneself to others. Thus, the chapter emphasises that the framework is not about fitting into what might be perceived as the 'right' or 'wrong' category but rather about acquiring self-awareness regarding one's biases and influences. It is about stressing that everyone has biases rooted in their experiences and understanding that recognising these biases is crucial for making informed decisions. By identifying blind spots, individuals can address moments of self-doubt and criticism, ultimately leading to more thoughtful reflection and quicker awareness in relation to their decisions (referenced in Chapter 7). The EPPJ framework encourages individuals to understand their personal experiences and how these shape their professional judgements, reinforcing the idea that one's identity is shaped by both personal and professional experiences.

The testimonies shared by individuals who have used the tool reflect profound transformations in their lives, highlighting increased self-awareness and improved decision-making abilities. Many describe the tool as a source of ongoing reflection and personal growth, akin to a good book or movie that reveals new insights with each revisit.

Dr Weekes advocates that organisations adopt this model, emphasising that self-aware employees are more likely to make better decisions, contributing positively to organisational culture and efficiency. This chapter has asserted that all professional sectors could benefit from such a framework, as it is essential for enhancing both personal development and organisational effectiveness.

Furthermore, the chapter discussed the interplay between personal and professional life, challenging the notion that one can entirely separate the two. Instead, it advocated for a deeper understanding of how personal experiences influence work-related judgements and emotions. By encouraging individuals to reflect on their EPPJ category, the framework not only aids in professional decision-making but also promotes personal growth and well-being. This holistic framework suggests that self-awareness is not merely a professional asset but a vital component of overall quality of life, making it a necessary tool for individuals and organisations alike.

Key takeaways from this chapter

- Completing the EPPJ tool with its scoring process enables individuals to identify their EPPJ category, which provides a structured framework for self-reflection.

- Recognising how personal and professional experiences shape identity enables an individual to gain a deeper understanding of personal biases and decision-making influences, without the need for comparison with others.

- Engaging with the EPPJ automated report is a form of ongoing continuous personal development, which encourages continual reflection and growth, enabling individuals to revisit their insights and develop a more nuanced understanding of their judgements and decision-making processes over time.

- Organisations should consider implementing the EPPJ framework to promote self-awareness among employees, resulting in improved decision-making and a positive workplace culture.

Chapter 10 | A unified approach: the future of EPPJ within and across disciplines

Education is the passport to the future, for tomorrow belongs to those who prepare for it today.

Malcolm X (1970)

Introduction

Having already explored the EPPJ model as a framework designed to guide social workers in making reflective, informed and ethical decisions, the EPPJ model encourages practitioners to integrate both personal and professional insights, fostering a comprehensive approach to decision-making that considers the complexities and nuances inherent in social work practice. This model supports practitioners in critically evaluating their actions and assumptions, thereby promoting accountability and ethical integrity.

Central to effective social work are values and ethics, as these shape not only the practice but also the identity of the social worker. Social work is grounded in a commitment to social justice, respect for individual rights and the promotion of human dignity. Therefore, an understanding and respect for difference and diversity are essential, as they enable social workers to appreciate and respond to the unique experiences, backgrounds and needs of everyone they serve. The Professional Capabilities Framework (PCF) outlines core skills and attributes required for effective practice, while legislative frameworks provide a legal structure within which social workers must operate, ensuring accountability and safeguarding rights.

This chapter explores how the EPPJ model can support effective decision-making across these areas, highlighting its relevance for ethical, reflective and values-driven social work practice, along with its wider application to higher education and other professional settings.

Values and ethics in social work through the EPPJ model

Values and ethics are foundational to social work, guiding practitioners in their interactions and decision-making processes. The British Association of Social Workers (BASW) Code of Ethics (BASW, 2021) sets out core ethical principles such as respect, integrity and a commitment to social justice. These values ensure that social workers should uphold the dignity and rights of individuals, fostering trust and accountability in their professional relationships. By adhering to these ethical standards, social workers navigate complex situations with a clear moral compass, ensuring their actions consistently reflect both personal and professional integrity.

Values play a pivotal role in shaping the judgements social workers make regarding what is right and ethical. Weekes (2023) highlights that personal and professional values function as a moral guide, influencing how social workers assess situations, prioritise client needs and determine appropriate interventions. This alignment between individual values and professional ethics is crucial for maintaining consistency, accountability and trustworthiness in social work practice. It ensures that decisions are not only legally compliant but also ethically sound, promoting the well-being and empowerment of clients.

Applying the EPPJ model to values and ethics

Effective judgement involves a deep understanding of both the social context and the specific details of each case. Values such as respect for autonomy, dignity and empowerment are essential in guiding decisions towards inclusive and anti-oppressive practices (Harris, 1987). By prioritising these values, social workers ensure that their interventions honour the client's self-determination and promote equitable outcomes. This approach helps to create environments where clients feel valued and supported, thereby enhancing the effectiveness of social work interventions.

A social worker's personal values, experiences and biases can significantly influence their interpretation of ethical standards. All the models identified in Chapter 8 underscore the importance of personal reflection in recognising and mitigating these biases. The cycle involves experiencing a situation, reflecting on the experience, conceptualising insights and planning future actions. Through this continuous process, social workers can enhance their self-awareness, minimise subjective biases and achieve greater objectivity in their ethical decision-making. This reflective practice ensures that personal beliefs do not overshadow professional responsibilities, fostering a more balanced and fair approach to client interactions.

Professional judgement requires aligning personal beliefs with organisational and professional standards (Social Work England, 2021). Social workers frequently encounter ethical dilemmas where they must balance their own values with the guidelines set forth by professional codes and the needs of their clients (Banks, 2020). In such scenarios, prioritising professional codes of ethics and the welfare of clients is essential for resolving conflicts. This alignment ensures that decisions are ethically sound and professionally appropriate, maintaining the integrity of the social work profession and safeguarding client interests.

Difference and diversity in social work through the EPPJ model

Understanding and embracing diversity and difference are essential in social work practice, as these elements shape the experiences and identities of clients and communities. According to the BASW Code of Ethics (BASW, 2021), social workers have a responsibility to respect and respond to the diversity of people and promote inclusivity and equity. Thompson's (2017) PCS Model provides a structured approach to understanding diversity across three levels: personal, cultural and structural. The personal level considers individual characteristics, experiences and identity; the cultural level addresses shared beliefs, norms and practices within groups; and the structural level examines the impact of social institutions and power dynamics. These interconnected dimensions of diversity highlight the multiple factors shaping individuals' lives and are crucial to social work practice.

Diversity is essential for promoting equity and inclusion, as it enables social workers to better appreciate and respond to clients' unique needs and challenges. Dalrymple and Burke (2019) emphasise that an informed approach to diversity helps practitioners actively work against discrimination, thus supporting inclusive practice and equitable outcomes. By understanding difference, social workers can create an environment where clients feel valued and understood, enhancing the quality of care and support they receive.

Applying the EPPJ model to difference and diversity

Effective judgement in social work requires an acute awareness of cultural humility and biases. Dominelli (2009) asserts that cultural humility – an understanding of cultural differences and the skills to interact effectively across them – strengthens effective judgement by equipping social workers with the knowledge and sensitivity needed to engage meaningfully with diverse clients. By being aware of and responding to cultural contexts, social workers are better able to support individuals in ways that are respectful, inclusive and free from assumptions. This cultural awareness and humility also aids in making judgements that acknowledge and address systemic inequalities, fostering anti-oppressive practice.

A social worker's own background, beliefs and biases can shape how they engage with difference. Reflexivity, as discussed in Chapter 8, involves critically examining one's own beliefs and assumptions in relation to practice. Reflexive practice encourages social workers to recognise how their personal histories may influence their perceptions and actions, helping to minimise biases. Regular supervision also plays a critical role in this process, providing a structured space for reflection and professional guidance. By continually engaging in reflexivity and supervision, social workers can better address their biases and engage with clients in a fair, open-minded manner.

Professionalism in social work includes a commitment to anti-discriminatory practice, a fundamental aspect of the PCF and the BASW Code of Ethics. This commitment requires practitioners to challenge discrimination actively, whether overt or subtle, in all forms. Thompson (2017) highlights that professional judgement involves balancing personal beliefs with organisational and professional standards to maintain client-centred care. By prioritising ethical principles and standards, social workers can mediate personal biases, ensuring that their practice is inclusive and respectful of each client's unique background and identity.

The Professional Capabilities Framework (PCF) and the EPPJ model

The PCF is the primary competency framework guiding social work practice in the United Kingdom. Developed by the BASW (2018), the PCF outlines nine domains that reflect the essential skills, values and knowledge required for effective social work practice. These domains include:

1. professionalism;
2. values and ethics;
3. diversity and equality;
4. rights, justice and economic well-being;
5. knowledge;
6. critical reflection and analysis;
7. intervention and skills;
8. contexts and organisations;
9. professional leadership.

Together, these domains provide a holistic framework for social workers to develop their practice, ensuring accountability, ethical integrity and client-centred care.

Applying the EPPJ model to PCF competencies

Each PCF domain demands effective judgement, as social workers must apply their skills thoughtfully and adaptively to varied contexts. For example, in the critical reflection and analysis domain, effective judgement is essential for using evidence-based approaches to assess situations accurately and address biases. This domain emphasises critical thinking, encouraging social workers to draw on research, evaluate information critically, and make decisions grounded in best practices. Effective judgement therefore ensures that social workers' interventions are well informed, client-centred and adaptable to each unique situation.

Personal judgement, shaped by self-awareness and reflexivity, is closely aligned with the values and ethics and rights, justice and economic well-being domains. These domains require social workers to examine their own values and beliefs and consider how these might impact their practice. Through personal judgement, social workers recognise and manage the influence of their personal experiences on their professional decisions, helping them uphold fairness and equity. By engaging in reflexive practice, social workers better understand how their own perspectives and biases may shape their interactions with clients, thus promoting ethical and just outcomes.

Professional judgement is integral to the professionalism and knowledge domains, as it involves aligning one's actions with professional standards and the broader social work knowledge base. In these domains, social workers must use professional knowledge and skills to navigate complex ethical situations and balance personal beliefs with client needs and ethical codes. Professionalism requires a commitment to ongoing learning, while the knowledge domain encourages the application of theoretical insights to inform practice. Through professional judgement, social workers bridge personal beliefs and professional responsibilities, ensuring that their practice remains ethical, informed and client-centred.

Legislative frameworks and the EPPJ model

In the United Kingdom, several key Acts provide a foundation for anti-discriminatory practice in social work. One of the most significant is the *Equality Act 2010*, which consolidates previous anti-discrimination laws and establishes a legal duty to protect individuals from discrimination based on protected characteristics such as race, gender, disability and sexual orientation. This Act shapes social work practice by requiring practitioners to actively challenge discrimination and promote inclusivity. Additionally, legislation such as the *Human Rights Act 1998* ensures that social workers uphold fundamental rights such as privacy, freedom and protection from harm, reinforcing the need for ethical and equitable practice (Evans and Harvey, 2022). Together, these laws serve as a legal and ethical framework, guiding social workers in fostering fairness, justice and respect for diversity.

Applying the EPPJ model to legislative frameworks

Effective judgement in the context of legislative frameworks involves a clear understanding of legal obligations related to anti-discriminatory practice and human rights. Social workers must be well versed in the requirements of the *Equality Act 2010* and other relevant legislation, ensuring that their decisions and actions align with these standards. This includes actively challenging discriminatory practices, promoting fair treatment and advocating for clients' rights. By making informed judgements, social workers can better fulfil their responsibility to protect clients from discrimination and uphold their dignity and autonomy.

Personal judgement in social work requires a commitment to aligning one's beliefs with the principles set out in relevant legislation. Social workers must reflect on, and where necessary adjust, their personal beliefs to ensure they do not conflict with legal mandates promoting equality and justice. Reflective practice enables social workers to recognise and address any biases, ensuring that personal views do not interfere with their obligation to treat all clients fairly and respectfully. Through this alignment, social workers foster an inclusive approach that upholds the core values of equality and non-discrimination.

Professional judgement is essential to applying legal knowledge in ways that promote clients' rights and ensure fair and respectful treatment. According to Banks (2020), this requires social workers to interpret and apply legislation to meet the needs of clients effectively and ethically. By prioritising inclusivity and fairness, social workers uphold the professional standards and ethical codes of the profession while honouring clients' rights and well-being. Professional judgement allows social workers to balance legal requirements with a client-centred approach, ensuring that practice is legally compliant, ethically sound and responsive to individual needs.

EPPJ in higher education (HE) and teaching

The EPPJ model plays a significant role in higher education, teaching and supervision within social work practice. This model provides a structured framework that supports students, educators and supervisors in cultivating essential skills for reflective, ethical and well-informed decision-making (Weekes, 2020). By promoting critical thinking and self-awareness, the EPPJ model prepares social work students and professionals to navigate the complex, value-laden situations they will encounter in practice.

Applying the EPPJ model to higher education and teaching

In higher education and teaching, the EPPJ model serves as a valuable tool for developing the judgement necessary for effective social work practice. Educators can use the model to guide students in understanding the interplay between personal beliefs, professional standards and ethical responsibilities (Weekes, 2023). The model encourages students to reflect on their own values and biases, aligning them with professional codes and ethical standards (Weekes, 2023). By embedding EPPJ in social work curricula, educators can foster the critical thinking and self-reflection essential for managing real-world challenges. This approach equips future practitioners to make balanced, client-centred decisions that are both informed and ethically sound.

In supervision within social work practice, the EPPJ model enhances the quality of reflective practice (see Chapter 8) and professional growth. Supervisors can use the model to guide practitioners through complex cases, helping them to explore the effective, personal and professional dimensions of their judgement. By encouraging social workers to engage in reflective practice, the model helps them identify and address any biases or assumptions that may influence their work. This reflective process is vital for developing self-awareness and ensuring that personal beliefs do not compromise professional integrity. Additionally, by reinforcing alignment with ethical and legal standards, the EPPJ model helps supervisors support practitioners in delivering ethically grounded and inclusive care.

Overall, the EPPJ model is instrumental in higher education, teaching and supervision, as it provides a structured approach for developing the reflective and ethical judgement that is central to effective social work practice. By embedding the principles of EPPJ in learning and supervision contexts, the model contributes to the development of skilled, self-aware and client-centred social workers capable of making thoughtful and ethically sound decisions.

EPPJ wider application

The EPPJ model has versatile applications beyond social work, offering value in fields such as health, business and finance. This model supports professionals in making balanced, ethical and well-informed decisions, especially in roles where the complexities of personal values, professional standards and effective decision-making converge. Although the previous chapters focused on social work, we assert that the model has application to other professions that overlap with social work, which can also have an impact on social workers and service-users. What follows is an overview of the professions to which it can apply.

Health

In healthcare, the EPPJ model can guide professionals in navigating ethical dilemmas, patient care decisions and team-based work. Healthcare decisions often require a balance of patient autonomy, clinical evidence and institutional guidelines.

Effective judgement

Healthcare professionals can use effective judgement to integrate clinical knowledge and best practices into their patient care decisions, balancing patient needs with available resources. For instance, effective judgement is essential in areas such as patient triage, where quick and informed decisions based on clinical urgency are required.

Personal judgement

Healthcare workers bring their own values and experiences to their roles, which can affect their views on treatment options, patient preferences and end-of-life care. Through personal judgement, guided by self-awareness, practitioners can reflect on and manage biases to ensure patient-centred care that respects diverse values.

Professional judgement

Professional judgement in healthcare requires adherence to medical ethics, legal standards and organisational policies. By grounding decisions in these standards, healthcare professionals can navigate challenges and resolve conflicts that may arise between their personal values and their duty to patients, prioritising client well-being and safety.

Police/courts and criminal justice settings

Effective judgement

Effective judgement focuses on achieving the best possible outcomes by integrating evidence-based practices, critical analysis and ethical considerations. In policing, officers often face high-pressure situations where quick, yet sound, decisions are essential. The EPPJ model encourages a balanced approach between instinctual responses and critical reflection, which can reduce instances of bias or misuse of authority (Weekes, 2021). For example, in the use of stop-and-search procedures, which have been criticised for disproportionately targeting global majority people (Home Office, 2021) and the adultification of young Black children (Davidson, 2018), applying effective judgement means assessing the legal grounds for the search while also considering the broader social implications. By doing so, officers are guided to make decisions that not only comply with the law but also uphold social justice, fairness and community trust.

In the courts, judges and magistrates use effective judgement when considering both static and dynamic risk factors in sentencing. The model promotes a holistic approach that goes beyond past convictions to include factors like evidence of rehabilitation and community support (Sentencing Council, 2022). This is particularly relevant for cases involving young offenders, where a focus on rehabilitative measures can lead to more positive long-term outcomes (Youth Justice Board, 2021). Thus, effective judgement in this context ensures that decisions are context-sensitive and tailored to the individual, ultimately contributing to more equitable sentencing.

Personal judgement

Personal judgement involves the use of individual values, self-awareness and reflective practice to guide decisions, especially in complex or ethically challenging situations. For police officers, personal judgement plays a crucial role in counteracting biases, especially in high-stakes scenarios such as stop-and-search. The EPPJ model fosters self-awareness, prompting officers to reflect on their personal biases and the ethical implications of their actions (College of Policing, 2020). By engaging in this reflective practice, officers can make more informed, unbiased decisions that align with principles of fairness and proportionality. This not only improves policing outcomes but also enhances community relations and trust.

In the judicial context, personal judgement is vital when judges exercise discretion. The EPPJ model supports judges in reflecting on the broader social context of each case, including the socioeconomic background of the defendant and any mitigating circumstances. This reflective approach ensures that personal values do not inadvertently influence sentencing, leading to more impartial and just outcomes. For instance, by acknowledging the impact of systemic inequalities, judges can make decisions that are more empathetic and socially aware, particularly in cases involving marginalised groups.

Professional judgement

Professional judgement is the application of ethical standards, legal frameworks and best practices within the criminal justice system. In policing, the EPPJ model aligns with professional standards by encouraging officers to apply both legal knowledge and ethical principles in their decision-making. For example, stop-and-search procedures must not only comply with statutory guidelines but also consider ethical implications and community impact. This approach helps to ensure that policing practices are both legally sound and socially responsible, thus reinforcing public trust.

In the courts, professional judgement is critical for upholding the integrity of the justice system. The EPPJ model helps judges balance the need for public safety with the rights of defendants, especially when using risk-assessment tools. By integrating qualitative judgements alongside quantitative assessments, such as the OASys tool used in probation and parole settings, the model ensures a more comprehensive evaluation of offenders (Ministry of Justice, 2020). This hybrid approach aligns with human rights obligations and promotes a fairer justice system (European Convention on Human Rights, 2021).

Impact on criminal justice policy and practice

In broader criminal justice settings, the EPPJ model can inform policy development, particularly around risk-assessment tools used in probation and parole settings. The model encourages practitioners to go beyond reliance on quantitative risk assessments, such as the Offender Assessment System, by incorporating qualitative judgements that account for individual circumstances (Ministry of Justice, 2020). This hybrid approach ensures that the rights of offenders are balanced with public safety considerations, aligning with human rights obligations (European Convention on Human Rights, 2021).

By fostering a reflective practice culture, the model also supports continuous professional development among criminal justice practitioners. It advocates for ongoing training in ethics and critical thinking, which is essential for maintaining public trust in the justice system (HM Inspectorate of Probation, 2023). For example, probation officers using the model can improve their engagement with service-users, leading to more effective rehabilitation and reduced recidivism rates.

Business

In business, the EPPJ model supports leaders and employees in ethical decision-making, conflict resolution and strategic planning. Ethical considerations and stakeholder impacts are crucial in business environments, and EPPJ can help professionals navigate these complexities.

Effective judgement

Business professionals need effective judgement to analyse data, market trends and financial implications in decision-making. This is essential when making decisions about investments, budgeting or resource allocation, to ensure choices are evidence-based and aligned with business goals.

Personal judgement

In business, personal judgement relates to the values, cultural perspectives and experiences of decision-makers. Reflecting on these factors can help professionals recognise how their background influences their business choices, improving objectivity and fairness in handling sensitive issues like workforce diversity and team dynamics.

Professional judgement

Professional judgement in business often involves upholding ethical standards, corporate social responsibility and regulatory compliance. Balancing profit motives with ethical practices, such as fair working standards or sustainable sourcing, requires professionals to prioritise long-term ethical standards over immediate financial gains, enhancing trust with customers and stakeholders.

Finance

In finance, the EPPJ model can help professionals navigate ethical issues in investment decisions, client relations and regulatory compliance. Financial decision-making often impacts clients' lives and requires a careful balance of professional knowledge, ethical principles and objectivity.

Effective judgement

Finance professionals rely on effective judgement to interpret data, evaluate risks and make strategic recommendations based on market conditions. Effective judgement helps ensure that investment advice or portfolio management is both sound and aligned with clients' financial goals and risk tolerance.

Personal judgement

Personal beliefs and values can influence how finance professionals view certain investments, industries and risk levels. By engaging in personal judgement, they can reflect on any biases that might affect their advice, ensuring that their personal preferences do not overshadow their clients' best interests.

Professional judgement

Professional judgement in finance involves adherence to industry standards, ethical guidelines and fiduciary duties. Finance professionals must apply their knowledge to uphold client trust, making choices that align with legal and ethical responsibilities, such as prioritising client interests and disclosing potential conflicts of interest.

Conclusion of EPPJ model

The EPPJ model is invaluable in supporting social workers to make well-rounded and reflective decisions across essential areas of practice, including values and ethics, diversity, the PCF and legislative frameworks. By structuring decision-making through three layers – effective, personal and professional judgement – the model enables practitioners to consider multiple perspectives and balance personal insights with professional standards and legal requirements.

In the area of values and ethics, the EPPJ model promotes thoughtful integration of ethical principles such as dignity, respect and social justice, helping social workers make decisions that are inclusive and aligned with core social work values. The model encourages self-awareness, enabling practitioners to recognise and address personal biases while also ensuring that they adhere to professional codes of conduct. Regarding diversity and difference, the EPPJ model emphasises cultural humility and reflexivity, supporting social workers in understanding and responding sensitively to each client's unique experiences and identity. This approach fosters anti-oppressive practice and helps practitioners create equitable and inclusive environments.

The model also aligns with the PCF competencies, guiding social workers in meeting the high standards of professionalism, reflection and knowledge application set out by the PCF domains. By balancing personal insights with the skills and values outlined in the PCF, social workers can deliver well-informed and client-centred care. Finally, within the framework of legislation, the EPPJ model ensures that social workers understand their legal obligations, including promoting equality and upholding human rights. By applying effective and professional judgement, social workers are better equipped to interpret and use legislation in ways that safeguard clients' rights and well-being.

The EPPJ model enhances reflective, ethical decision-making across diverse fields by helping professionals integrate personal insight, effective decision-making and professional standards. Whether in healthcare, business, finance or other areas, the EPPJ model supports ethically sound, client-centred and well-rounded decision-making, contributing to responsible and trustworthy practices across sectors.

Case study

Maria, a 72 year-old woman of South Asian descent, has recently been referred for adult social care due to mobility issues and increasing difficulties managing her daily activities. She lives with her son and his family, who are actively involved in her care. Maria's cultural background places significant emphasis on family care, and she has always maintained a traditional role within the family. However, Maria has expressed a desire for more independence and to receive care services outside of the family home, which has caused tension between her and her son, who feels it is his duty to care for her in line with cultural expectations.

Reflective exercise

Under the following headings, how would you apply the EPPJ model to this case?

Effective judgement

- Assessing needs
- Evidence-based decision-making
- Conflict resolution

Personal judgement

- Self-awareness
- Reflexivity
- Empathy

Professional judgement

- Adherence to professional codes
- Advocacy
- Balancing client and family needs

Capture personal reflections and individual thoughts

» Critically reflect on this chapter and what you have learned and record your own personal thoughts and feelings.

Chapter summary

This chapter has explored the application of the EPPJ model in social work practice, along with a number of other professional backgrounds, focusing on its role in guiding decision-making across various critical areas: values and ethics, diversity, the PCF and legislative frameworks. The EPPJ model encourages reflective, ethical and informed decision-making by integrating both personal and professional insights. This helps social workers critically evaluate their actions and assumptions, fostering accountability, promoting human dignity and supporting inclusive and anti-oppressive practices. The chapter emphasised the importance of values, ethics, diversity, professional capabilities and legal frameworks in shaping social work practice and explored how the EPPJ model can support social workers in navigating complex, value-laden situations to make ethical and client-centred decisions.

Key takeaways from this chapter

- The EPPJ model encourages social workers and other professionals to integrate personal experiences, values and biases with professional codes and standards, ensuring decisions are ethically sound and client-centred.

- Core values such as respect for autonomy, dignity and empowerment play a central role in guiding social workers' and other professionals' ethical decision-making, ensuring their actions are in alignment with different professional codes of ethics.

- The EPPJ model highlights the importance of cultural humility, ensuring social workers and other professionals are aware of biases and able to engage with diverse clients in ways that promote inclusivity, anti-oppressive practices and respect for diversity.

- The chapter emphasises that professional judgement requires social workers and other professionals to actively challenge discrimination and uphold the values of equality and justice, as outlined in the PCF and legislative frameworks such as the *Equality Act 2010*.

- Reflective practices, such as Kolb's reflective cycle and regular supervision, are essential for helping social workers and other professionals recognise and address personal biases, thereby enhancing their ability to make fair, balanced and professional judgements in complex situations.
- EPPJ is applicable across a wider range of disciplines outside of social work practice.

Glossary

A

Agnosticism: The belief that the existence of God or the divine is unknown or unknowable.

Almsgiving: The act of giving to the poor and needy, common in many religions.

Atheism: The lack of belief in the existence of God or gods.

B

Brahman: In Hinduism, the ultimate reality or cosmic spirit.

C

Clergy: Individuals ordained for religious duties, such as priests, ministers and imams.

Covenant: A solemn agreement between God and a group of people, common in Judaism and Christianity.

Cult: A religious group with beliefs or practices that are often considered outside the mainstream.

D

Dharma: In Hinduism and Buddhism, the moral law combined with spiritual discipline that guides one's life.

Doctrine: A set of beliefs or teachings held and promoted by a religious group.

E

Ecumenical: Relating to the promotion of unity among the world's Christian churches. The term often refers to efforts, dialogues and movements aimed at fostering cooperation and understanding among different Christian denominations.

Episcopal: Relating to a system of church government by bishops, found in certain Christian denominations.

F

Fable: A short story, typically with a moral lesson, often featuring animals as characters.

Faithful: Loyal and steadfast in beliefs or allegiances, often referring to adherence to religious principles.

Fellowship: A community of individuals sharing common religious beliefs or practices.

Fundamentalism: A strict adherence to specific theological doctrines, often reacting against modern interpretations of faith.

G

Gnosticism: A collection of ancient religions with beliefs centred around occult knowledge and spiritual enlightenment.

Guru: A spiritual teacher or guide in Hinduism and Buddhism.

H

Holiness: The state of being holy, often associated with purity and separation from sin.

I

Immanence: The belief that the divine is present and active within the world.

J

Jihad: In Islam, a term often interpreted as 'struggle' or 'striving', encompassing personal and communal efforts to live according to God's will.

Jinn: Supernatural beings in Islamic theology, often considered to have free will and capable of good or evil.

K

Kaaba: A sacred structure located in Mecca, Saudi Arabia, which is the most important site in Islam and the direction towards which Muslims pray.

Kirtan: A form of devotional singing in Hinduism, often involving call-and-response chanting of hymns and mantras.

L

Liturgical: Pertaining to public worship and the prescribed order of service in a religious context. This includes the rituals, prayers, readings and ceremonies that structure the worship experience in various religious traditions, particularly within Christianity.

M

Meditation: A practice of focused attention, often used in various religious traditions for spiritual growth and inner peace.

Monotheism/ monotheistic: The belief in a single, all-powerful God.

Mythology: A collection of myths, especially one belonging to a particular religious or cultural tradition, often involving multiple gods.

N

New Age: A broad movement encompassing various spiritual and metaphysical beliefs that emerged in the late twentieth century.

Nirvana: In Buddhism, the ultimate state of liberation and freedom from suffering.

O

Opus Dei: A personal prelature of the Roman Catholic Church that emphasises the pursuit of holiness in everyday life.

Orthodox: Referring to traditional or established beliefs that adhere to established doctrines.

P

Paganism: A term for various polytheistic, nature-based religions, often outside of the Abrahamic faiths.

Pantheon: The collective deities of a particular religion, often representing various aspects of life and nature.

Pilgrimage: A journey to a sacred place or shrine, common in many religious traditions.

Puja: A Hindu ritual of worship, involving offerings and prayers.

Q

Qibla: The direction in which Muslims face during prayer, which is towards the Kaaba in Mecca.

Quaker: A member of the Religious Society of Friends, known for their commitment to peace, simplicity and social justice.

R

Revelation: The act of revealing divine truth or knowledge, often through sacred texts or prophetic figures.

Ritual: A formalised ceremony, often religious, that involves a prescribed sequence of actions.

S

Samsara: In Hinduism and Buddhism, the cycle of birth, death and rebirth.

Scripture: Sacred writings considered authoritative in a particular religion.

Shaman: A spiritual leader or healer in many Indigenous and polytheistic cultures, believed to communicate with the spirit world.

Sharia: Islamic law derived from the Quran and Hadith, governing all aspects of a Muslim's life.

Syncretism: The blending of different religious beliefs and practices.

T

Theism: The belief in the existence of a God or gods.

Thetan: For Scientologists, the Thetan is the immortal spiritual being or soul, the true self, existing beyond physical death and reincarnating across lifetimes.

Transcendence: The aspect of the divine that is beyond the physical universe.

U

Universalism: The belief that all people will ultimately be saved or that all religions lead to the same truth.

V

Veneration: Great respect or reverence for a person, often associated with saints or holy figures in various traditions.

Virtue: Moral excellence and righteousness; behaviour showing high moral standards.

Z

Zakat: A form of almsgiving treated in Islam as a religious obligation, typically involving a percentage of one's wealth given to charity.

Zealot: A person who is fanatical and uncompromising in pursuit of their religious, political or other ideals.

Zen: A school of Mahayana Buddhism that emphasises meditation and direct experience.

References

Abelson, R P and Levi, A (1985) Decision Making and Decision Theory. In Lindzey, G E and Aronson, E E (eds) *Handbook of Social Psychology*, 3rd ed. (pp 231–309). New York: Random House.

Alfandari, R, Taylor, B J, Enosh, G, Killick, C et al (2023) Group Decision-making Theories for Child and Family Social Work. *European Journal of Social Work*, 26(2): 204–17.

Bailey, M (2010) *Misogynoir in Media: The Role of Race and Gender in Portrayals of Black Women*. [online] Available at: https://example-link.com (accessed 23 September 2024).

Bakay, A, Huang, J and Huang, Y (2014) Group Decision-making Processes and Group Decision Quality: Moderation of Mutual Interest. *International Journal of Management and Decision Making*, 13(4): 335–55.

Banks, S (2020) *Ethical Issues in Social Work Practice*, 2nd ed. Basingstoke: Palgrave Macmillan.

Baron, J (1994) *Thinking and Deciding*, 2nd ed. Cambridge: Cambridge University Press.

Bawden, D and Robinson, L (2009) The Dark Side of Information: Overload, Anxiety and Other Paradoxes and Pathologies. *Journal of Information Science*, 35(2): 180–91.

Bechara, A, Damasio, H, Tranel, D and Damasio, A R (2000) The Iowa Gambling Task and the Somatic Marker Hypothesis: Some Questions and Answers. *Trends in Cognitive Sciences*, 9(4): 159–62.

Beck, U and Beck-Gernsheim, E (2002) *Individualization: Institutionalized Individualism and its Social and Political Consequences*. London: SAGE.

Becker, G S (1976) *The Economic Approach to Human Behaviour*. Chicago, IL: University of Chicago Press.

Becker, H (1963) *Outsiders: Studies in the Sociology of Deviance*. New York: The Free Press.

Biestek, F P (1953) The Non-judgmental Attitude. *Social Casework*, 34(6): 235–9.

Bion, R (1962) *Learning from Experience*. London: Heinemann.

Bion, W (1988) A Theory of Thinking. In Bott Spillius, E (ed) *Melanie Klein Today: Developments in Theory and Practice: Volume 1 Mainly Theory* (pp 178–86). London: Routledge.

Blumer, H (1986) *Symbolic Interactionism: Perspective and Method*. Berkeley, CA: University of California Press.

Bodenhausen, G V and Wyer, R Jr (1985) Effects of Stereotypes on Decision-making and Information Processing Strategies. *Journal of Personality and Social Psychology*, 48(2): 267–82.

Bolen, J (1989) *Gods in Everyman*. San Francisco, CA: Harper and Row.

Bornstein, B H and Greene, E (2011) Jury Decision Making: Implications for and from Psychology. *Current Directions in Psychological Science*, 20(1): 63–7. https://doi.org/10.1177/0963721410397282.

Bornstein, B H and Miller, M K (2009) Does a Judge's Religion Influence Decision Making?, *Court Review*, 45(3): 112–15.

Borton, T (1970) *Reach, Teach and Touch*. New York: McGraw Hill.

Boud, D, Keogh, R and Walker, D (1985) Promoting Reflection in Learning: A Model. In Boud, D, Keogh, R and Walker, D (eds) *Reflection: Turning Experience into Learning* (pp 18–40). London: Routledge.

Bratt, C, Abrams, D and Swift, H J (2020) Supporting the Old but Neglecting the Young? The Two Faces of Ageism. *Developmental Psychology*, 56(5): 1029–39. https://doi.org/10.1037/dev0000903.

Bressen, T (2007) Consensus Decision Making. In Holman, P, Devane, T and Cady, S (eds) *The Change Handbook: The Definitive Resource on Today's Best Methods for Engaging Whole Systems* (pp 212–17). San Francisco, CA: Berrett-Koehler.

REFERENCES

British Association of Social Workers (BASW) (2018) *Professional Capabilities Framework (PCF).* [online] Available at: www.basw.co.uk/professional-development/professional-capabilities-framework-pcf/the-pcf (accessed 6 November 2024).

British Association of Social Workers (BASW) (2021) *Code of Ethics for Social Work: Statement of Ethical Principles.* [online] Available at: www.basw.co.uk/code-ethics (accessed 6 November 2024).

Brookfield, S (1988) *Training Educators of Adults: The Theory and Practice of Graduate Adult Education.* New York: Routledge.

Brown, M E and Treviño, L K (2006) Ethical Leadership: A Review and Future Directions. *The Leadership Quarterly*, 17(6): 595–616.

Brynjolfsson, E and McAfee, A (2014) *The Second Machine Age: Work, Progress, and Prosperity in a Time of Brilliant Technologies.* New York: W W Norton.

Butler, J (1990) *Gender Trouble: Feminism and the Subversion of Identity.* London: Routledge.

Carlson, K A and Russo, J E (2001) Biased Interpretation of Evidence by Mock Jurors. *Journal of Experimental Psychology: Applied*, 7(2): 91–103. https://doi.org/10.1037//1076-898X.7.2.91.

Carmichael, S and Hamilton, C V (1967) *Black Power: The Politics of Liberation.* New York: Vintage.

Carroll, A B (1991) The Pyramid of Corporate Social Responsibility: Toward the Moral Management of Organizational Stakeholders. *Business Horizons*, 34(4): 39–48.

Cheng, K E and Deek, F P (2012) Voting Tools in Group Decision Support Systems: Theory and Implementation. *International Journal of Management and Decision Making*, 12(1): 1–20.

Chidiac, D (2013) *Who Says You Can't? You Do: The Life-Changing Self-Help Book that's Empowering People Around the World to Live an Extraordinary Life.* London: John Murray Press.

Children Act 2004 (2004) [online] Available at: www.legislation.gov.uk/ukpga/2004/31/contents (accessed 17 October 2023).

Cialdini, R B and Goldstein, N J (2004) Social Influence: Compliance and Conformity. *Annual Review of Psychology*, 55: 591–621.

College of Policing (2020) *Code of Ethics: A Code of Practice for the Principles and Standards of Professional Behaviour for the Policing Profession of England and Wales.* London: College of Policing.

Collins, D, Jordan, C and Coleman, H (2010) *An Introduction to Family Social Work*, 3rd ed. Belmont, CA: Brooks/Cole.

Collins, P H (1996) What's in a Name? Womanism, Black Feminism, and Beyond. *The Black Scholar*, 26(1): 9–17. https://doi.org/10.1080/00064246.1996.11430765.

Costa, P T Jr and McCrae, R R (1992) *Revised NEO Personality Inventory (NEO-PI-R) and NEO Five-Factor Inventory (NEO-FFI) Professional Manual.* Lutz, FL: Psychological Assessment Resources.

Crenshaw, K (1989) Demarginalizing the Intersection of Race and Sex: A Black Feminist Critique of Anti-Discrimination Doctrine, Feminist Theory and Antiracist Politics. *University of Chicago Legal Forum*, 1: 139–67.

Cumming, E and Henry, W E (1961) *Growing Old: The Process of Disengagement.* New York: Basic Books.

Cupich, B J (2015) Op Ed in *Chicago Tribune.* Chicago Catholic, 10 August. [online] Available at: https://www.chicagocatholic.com/cardinal-blase-j.-cupich/-/article/2015/08/10/op-ed-in-chicago-tribune (accessed 2 April 2025).

Dalrymple, J and Burke, B (2019) *Anti-Oppressive Practice: Social Care and the Law*, 4th ed. Maidenhead: Open University Press.

Damasio, A R (1994) *Descartes' Error: Emotion, Reason, and the Human Brain.* New York: G P Putnam's Sons.

Davies, A J H (2018) *The Impact of Adultification on Black Children in Schools*. London: Routledge.

Davis, J H, Stasson, M F, Ôno, K and Zimmerman, S K (1988) Effects of Straw Polls on Group Decision Making: Sequential Voting Pattern, Timing, and Local Majorities. *Journal of Personality and Social Psychology*, 55(6): 918–26. https://doi.org/10.1037/0022-3514.55.6.918.

De Bortoli, L and Dolan, M (2015) Decision Making in Social Work with Families and Children: Developing Decision-Aids Compatible with Cognition. *British Journal of Social Work*, 45(7): 2142–60.

de la Fuente-Núñez, V, Cohn-Schwartz, E, Roy, S and Ayalon, L (2021) Scoping Review on Ageism against Younger Populations. *International Journal of Environmental Research and Public Health*, 18(8): 3988. https://doi.org/10.3390/ijerph18083988.

Deal, T E and Kennedy, A A (1982) *Corporate Cultures: The Rites and Rituals of Corporate Life*. Boston, MA: Addison-Wesley.

Delgado, R and Stefancic, J (2001) *Critical Race Theory: An Introduction*. New York: New York University Press.

Dewey, J (1938) *Experience and Education*. New York: Macmillan.

Dominelli, L (2009) Anti-Oppressive Practice: The Challenges of the Twenty-First Century. In Adams, R, Dominelli, L and Payne, M (eds) *Social Work: Themes, Issues and Debates*, 3rd ed. (pp 49–64). Basingstoke: Palgrave Macmillan.

Dourish, P and Bellotti, V (1992) Awareness and Coordination in Shared Workspaces. In *Proceedings of the 1992 ACM Conference on Computer-Supported Cooperative Work, CSCW '92* (pp 107–14). New York: ACM.

Dowley, T and Partridge, C H (2018) *A Short Introduction to World Religions*. Minneapolis, MN: Fortress Press.

Driscoll, J (2007) Reflective Practice for Practise. *Senior Nurse*, 13: 47–50.

Durkheim, E (1997 [1884]) *The Division of Labor in Society*. New York: The Free Press.

Erikson, E H (1950) *Childhood and Society*. New York: W W Norton.

European Convention on Human Rights (2021) The Hague: Council of Europe.

Evans, M and Harvey, D (2022) *Social Work Law: Applying the Law in Practice*. St Albans: Critical Publishing.

Facione, P A (1990) *Critical Thinking: A Statement of Expert Consensus for Purposes of Educational Assessment and Instruction*. Newark, DE: American Philosophical Association.

Fanon, F (1961) *The Wretched of the Earth*. Harmondsworth: Penguin.

Fanon, F (2021) *Black Skin, White Masks*. Harmondsworth: Penguin.

Felitti, V, Anda, R, Nordenberg, D, Williamson, D F et al (1998) Relationship of Childhood Abuse and Household Dysfunction to Many of the Leading Causes of Death in Adults. The Adverse Childhood Experiences (ACE) Study. *American Journal of Preventative Medicine*, 14(4): 245–58.

Finlay, L (2008) *Reflecting on 'Reflective Practice'*. Maidenhead: The Open University.

Fook, J (2002) *Social Work: Critical Theory and Practice*. London: Sage.

Forrester, D, Westlake, D, McCann, M, Thurnham, A et al (2013) *Reclaiming Social Work? An Evaluation of System Units as an Approach to Delivering Children's Services*. Luton: University of Bedfordshire.

Forsyth, D R (2006) Decision making. In *Group Dynamics*, 5th ed. (pp 317–49). Belmont, CA: Cengage Learning.

Freeman, R E (1984) *Strategic Management: A Stakeholder Approach*. Lanham, MD: Pitman.

Freire, P (1970) *Pedagogy of the Oppressed*. New York: Continuum.

Freud, S (1899) *The Interpretation of Dreams*. London: Hogarth Press.

REFERENCES

Freud, S (1901) *The Psychopathology of Everyday Life*. London: Hogarth Press.

Gibbs, G (1988) *Learning by Doing: A Guide to Teaching and Learning Methods*. Oxford: Oxford Polytechnic.

Giddens, A (1992) *The Transformation of Intimacy: Sexuality, Love, and Eroticism in Modern Societies*. Stanford, CA: Stanford University Press.

Gigerenzer, G and Gaissmaier, W (2011) Heuristic Decision Making. *Annual Review of Psychology*, 62: 451–82.

Gilbert, P and Stickley, T (2012) 'Wounded Healers': The Role of Lived Experience in Mental Health Education and Practice. *The Journal of Mental Health Training, Education and Practice*, 7(1): 33–41. https://doi.org/10.1108/17556221211230570.

Gladwell, M (2005) *Blink: The Power of Thinking Without Thinking*. New York: Little, Brown and Company.

Gledhill, S (2021) *F.A.I.T.H. Assessment Tool*. London.

Goleman, D (1995) *Emotional Intelligence: Why It Can Matter More than IQ*. New York: Bantam Books.

Grant, L and Kinman, G (2015) Online Guide to Developing Emotional Resilience. [online] Available at: ccinform.co.uk (accessed 1 October 2024).

Halberstam, J (1998) *Female Masculinity*. Durham, NC: Duke University Press.

Hammond, K (1996) *Human Judgement and Social Policy*. Oxford: Oxford University Press.

Harris, N (1987) Defensive Social Work. *The British Journal of Social Work*, 17(1): 61–9. [online] Available at: www.jstor.org/stable/23707214 (accessed 7 February 2025).

Harvey, D and Weeks, A P (2023) Managing Risk and Decision-Making Processes. In Taylor, B (ed) *The Sage Handbook of Decision Making, Assessment and Risk in Social Work* (pp 535–45). Thousand Oaks, CA: Sage.

Haslam, S A (2004) *Psychology in Organizations*. London: Sage.

Hastie, R and Kameda, T (2005) The Robust Beauty of Majority Rules in Group Decisions. *Psychological Review*, 112(2): 494–508. https://doi.org/10.1037/0033-295x.112.2.494.

Haughton, S, Tucher, C and Harvey, D (2023) The Role of Reflection in Breaking the Cycle of Unsafe Practice. In Mantell, A and Scragg, T (eds) *Reflective Practice in Social Work* (pp 106–26). Thousand Oaks, CA: Sage.

Havighurst, R J (1961) Successful Aging. *The Gerontologist*, 1(1): 8–13. https://doi.org/10.1093/geront/1.1.8.

HM Inspectorate of Probation (2023) *Annual Report: Quality and Effectiveness of Probation Services*. London: HMIP.

Hofstede, G (1980) *Culture's Consequences: International Differences in Work-Related Values*. Thousand Oaks, CA: Sage.

Home Office (2021) *Police Powers and Procedures: Stop and Search Statistics, England and Wales, Year Ending March 2021*. London: Home Office.

hooks, b (2000) *Feminist Theory: From Margin to Centre*. Boston, MA: South End Press.

hooks, b (2014) *'Ain't I a Woman?' Black Women and Feminism*. London: Routledge.

Housley, W (2003) *Interaction in Multidisciplinary Teams*. Aldershot: Ashgate.

Hsu, L C (2014) A Hybrid Multiple Criteria Decision-making Model for Investment Decision Making. *Journal of Business Economics and Management*, 15(3): 509–29.

Isen, A M (2001) An Influence of Positive Affect on Decision Making in Complex Situations: Theoretical Issues with Practical Implications. *Journal of Consumer Psychology*, 11(2): 75–85.

Jackson, S W (2001) The Wounded Healer. *Bulletin of the History of Medicine*, 75(1): 1–36. https://doi.org/10.1353/bhm.2001.0025.

James, C L R (2023) *The Black Jacobins: Toussaint L'Ouverture and the San Domingo Revolution.* Harmondsworth: Penguin.

Janis, I (1971) Groupthink. *Psychology Today*, 5(6): 43–6.

Janis, I (1972) *Victims of Groupthink: A Psychological Study of Foreign-Policy Decisions and Fiascoes.* Boston, MA: Houghton Mifflin.

Janis, I (1982) *Groupthink: Psychological Studies of Policy Decisions and Fiascos*, 2nd ed. Boston, MA: Houghton Mifflin.

Johnston, M A and Paulsen, N (2014) Rules of Engagement: A Discrete Choice Analysis of Sponsorship Decision Making. *Journal of Marketing Management*, 30(7–8): 634–63.

Judge, T A and Ilies, R (2002) Relationship of Personality to Performance Motivation: A Meta-analytic Review. *Journal of Applied Psychology*, 87(4): 797–807.

Jung, C G (1961) *Memories, Dreams and Reflections.* London: Fontana.

Jung, C G (1993) *The Practice of Psychotherapy*, 2nd ed. London: Routledge.

Kahneman, D (2011) *Thinking, Fast and Slow.* New York: Farrar, Straus, and Giroux.

Kant, I (1785) *Groundwork of the Metaphysics of Morals.* Cambridge: Cambridge University Press.

Kerr, N L and Tindale, R S (2004) Group Performance and Decision Making. *Annual Review of Psychology*, 55: 623–56.

Killian, J and Todnem, G (1991) Reflective Judgement Concepts of Justification and Their Relationship to Age and Education. *Journal of Applied Developmental Psychology*, 2(2): 89–116.

Klein, G (2008) Naturalistic Decision Making. *Human Factors*, 50(3): 456–60.

Klein, M (1975) *Envy and Gratitude and Other Works 1946–1963.* London: Hogarth Press and Institute of Psychoanalysis.

Klein, M (2012) Notes on Some Schizoid Mechanisms. In Spillius, E and O'Shaughnessy, E (eds) *Projective Identification: The Fate of a Concept* (pp 19–46). London: Routledge.

Klimek, P, Hanel, R and Thurner, S (2009) Parkinson's Law Quantified: Three Investigations on Bureaucratic Inefficiency. *Journal of Statistical Mechanics: Theory and Experiment*, 3: P03008.

Kolb, D A (1984) *Experiential Learning: Experience as the Source of Learning and Development.* Englewood Cliffs, NJ: Prentice-Hall.

Korthagen, F and Vasalos, A (2005) Levels in Reflection: Core Reflection as a Means to Enhance Professional Growth. *Teachers and Teaching*, 11(1): 47–71. https://doi.org/10.1080/1354060042000337093.

Laming, Lord (2003) *The Victoria Climbié Inquiry.* London: UK Parliament.

Larson, J R (2010) *In Search of Synergy in Small Group Performance.* Bristol: Psychology Press.

LeDoux, J E (2000) Emotion Circuits in the Brain. *Annual Review of Neuroscience*, 23(1): 155–84.

Lerner, J S and Keltner, D (2001) Fear, Anger, and Risk. *Journal of Personality and Social Psychology*, 81(1): 146–59.

Lev, A I (2004) *Transgender Emergence: Therapeutic Guidelines for Working with Gender-Variant People and Their Families.* Binghamton, NY: Haworth Press.

Levine, J M, Resnick, L B and Higgins, E T (1993) Social Foundations of Cognition. *Annual Review of Psychology*, 44(1): 585–612.

Link, B G and Phelan, J C (2001) Conceptualizing Stigma. *Annual Review of Sociology*, 27(1): 363–85.

REFERENCES

Lord, C, Ross, L and Lepper, M (1979) Biased Assimilation and Attitude Polarisation: The Effects of Prior Theories on Subsequently Considered Evidence. *Journal of Personality and Social Psychology*, 37(11): 2098–109. https://doi.org/10.1037/0022-3514.37.11.2098.

Lu, L, Yuan, Y C and McLeod, P (2011) Twenty-Five Years of Hidden Profiles in Group Decision Making. *Personality and Social Psychology Review*, 16(1): 54–75. http://doi.org/10.1177/1088868311417243.

Luft, J and Ingram, H (1955) *The Johari Window, a Graphic Model of Interpersonal Awareness*. Los Angeles, CA: California University of California Western Training Lab.

Mackay, T (2023) Lived Experience in Social Work: An Under-utilised Expertise. *The British Journal of Social Work*, 53(3): 18331840. https://doi.org/10.1093/bjsw/bcad028.

Maclean, S (2016) *Reflective Practice Cards: Prompt Cards for Social Workers*. Lichfield: Kirwen Maclean Associates.

Macpherson, W (1999) *The Stephen Lawrence Inquiry: Report of an Inquiry by Sir William Macpherson of Cluny*. London: HMSO.

Majolo, M, Gomes, W B and DeCastro, T G (2023) Self-Consciousness and Self-Awareness: Associations between Stable and Transitory Levels of Evidence. *Behavioral Sciences*, 13(2): 117. https://doi.org/10.3390/bs13020117.

Marx, K (1848) *The Communist Manifesto*. London: The Communist League.

McAdams, D P (1993) *The Stories We Live By: Personal Myths and the Making of the Self*. New York: William Morrow & Co.

McGowan, M (2018) Scott Morrison Sends His Children to Private School to Avoid 'Skin Curling' Sexuality Discussions. *The Guardian*, 3 September. [online] Available at: www.theguardian.com/australia-news/2018/sep/03/scott-morrison-sends-his-children-to-private-school-to-avoid-skin-curling-sexuality-discussions?CMP=share_btn_url (accessed 25 September 2024).

Mian, A and Sufi, A (2014) *House of Debt: How They (and You) Caused the Great Recession, and How We Can Prevent It from Happening Again*. Chicago, IL: University of Chicago Press.

Middleton, R (2017) Critical Reflection: The Struggle of a Practice Developer. *International Practice Development Journal*, 7(1): 4.1–4.6.

Mill, J S (1861) *Utilitarianism*. London: Parker, Son and Bourn.

Miller, E K and Cohen, J D (2001) An Integrative Theory of Prefrontal Cortex Function. *Annual Review of Neuroscience*, 24, 167–202.

Miller, P (2021) 'System Conditions', System Failure, Structural Racism and Anti-Racism in the United Kingdom: Evidence from Education and Beyond. *Societies*, 11(2): 42. https://doi.org/10.3390/soc11020042.

Ministry of Justice (2020) *Offender Assessment System (OASys) Manual*. London: Ministry of Justice.

Mintzberg, H (1979) *The Structuring of Organizations: A Synthesis of the Research*. Englewood Cliffs, NJ: Prentice-Hall.

Mintzberg, H (1980) Structure in 5s: A Synthesis of the Research on Organization Design. *Management Science*, 26(3): 322–41.

Montague, P R, Hyman, S E and Cohen, J D (2006) Computational Roles for Dopamine in Behavioural Control. *Nature*, 431(7010): 760–67.

Moore, D A and Healy, P J (2008) The Trouble with Overconfidence. *Psychological Review*, 115(2): 502–17.

Morrison, T (2005) *Staff Supervision in Social Care*. Brighton: Pavilion.

Morrison, T and Wonnacott, J (2010) *Supervision: Now or Never, Reclaiming Reflective Supervision in Social Work*. [online] Available at: www.in-trac.co.uk/supervision-now-or-never (accessed 2 August 2024).

Moscovici, S and Zavalloni, M (1969) The Group as a Polarizer of Attitudes. *Journal of Personality and Social Psychology*, 12(2): 125–35. https://doi.org/10.1037/h0027568.

Mugumbate, J and Nyanguru, A (2015) Exploring African Philosophy: The Value of Ubuntu in Social Work. *African Journal of Social Work*, 3(1): 82–100.

Nemeth, C J (1986) Differential Contributions of Majority and Minority Influence. *Psychological Review*, 93(1): 23–32.

Newcomb, M, Burton, J, Edwards, N and Hazelwood, Z (2015) How Jung's Concept of the Wounded Healer Can Guide Learning and Teaching in Social Work and Human Services. *Advances in Social Work and Welfare Education*, 17(2): 55–69.

Nguyen, Q D, Fernandez, N, Karsenti, T and Charlin, B (2014) What is Reflection? A Conceptual Analysis of Major Definitions and a Proposal of a Five-Component Model. *Medical Education*, 48(12): 1176–89. https://doi.org/10.1111/medu.12583.

Nickerson, R S (1998) Confirmation Bias: A Ubiquitous Phenomenon in Many Guises. *Review of General Psychology*, 2(2): 175–220.

Nietzsche, F (1883) *Thus Spoke Zarathustra*. Harmondsworth: Penguin.

Noss, D and Grangaard, B (2017) *A History of the World's Religions*, 14th ed. London: Routledge.

O'Sullivan, T (2011) *Decision Making in Social Work*, 2nd ed. Basingstoke: Palgrave Macmillan.

Oliver, M (1990) *The Politics of Disablement: A Sociological Approach*. New York: St Martin's Press.

Oruka, H O (1990) *Sage Philosophy: Indigenous Thinkers and Modern Debate on African Philosophy*. Leiden: Brill.

Oxhandler, H K, Parrish, D E, Torres, L R and Achenbaum, W A (2015) The Integration of Clients' Religion and Spirituality in Social Work Practice: A National Survey. *Social Work*, 60(3): 228–37. https://doi.org/10.1093/sw/swv018.

Parks, R (1990) Women of the Hall: Rosa Parks, *Women's National Hall of Fame*, 2 April. [online] Available at: https://libquotes.com/rosa-parks/quote/lbc2s8u (accessed 2 April 2025).

Parsons, T (1951) *The Social System*. New York: The Free Press.

Payne, J W, Bettman, J R and Johnson, E J (1993) *The Adaptive Decision Maker*. Cambridge: Cambridge University Press.

Pennington, N and Hastie, R (1992) Explaining the Evidence: Test of the Story Model for Jury Decision Making. *Journal of Personality and Social Psychology*, 62(2): 189–206. https://doi.org/10.1037/0022-3514.62.2.189.

Phelps, E A (2006) Emotion and Cognition: Insights from Studies of the Human Amygdala. *Annual Review of Psychology*, 57: 27–53.

Pigott, M A and Foley, L A (1995) Social Influence in Jury Decision Making. *Trial Diplomacy Journal*, 18: 101–8.

Platt, L (2014) The 'Wicked Problem' of Reflective Practice: A Critical Literature Review. *Innovations in Practice*, 9(1): 44–53.

Ptah-Hotep (c. 2400 BCE) *The Maxims of Ptah-Hotep*.

Ramose, M B (1999) *African Philosophy Through Ubuntu*. Harare: Mond Books.

Reamer, F G (2013) *Social Work Values and Ethics*, 4th ed. New York: Columbia University Press.

REFERENCES

Reason, J (1990) *Human Error*. Cambridge: Cambridge University Press.

Redish, A D, Jensen, S and Johnson, A (2008) A Unified Framework for Addiction: Vulnerabilities in the Decision Process. *Behavioral and Brain Sciences*, 31(4): 415–37.

Resnik, M D (2002) *Choices: An Introduction to Decision Theory*. Minneapolis, MN: University of Minnesota Press.

Roberts, B W, Chernyshenko, O S, Stark, S and Goldberg, L R (2009) The Structure of Conscientiousness: An Empirical Investigation Based on Seven Major Personality Questionnaires. *Personnel Psychology*, 58(1): 103–39.

Rolfe, G, Freshwater, D and Jasper, M (2001) *Critical Reflection in Nursing and the Helping Professions: A User's Guide*. Basingstoke: Palgrave Macmillan.

Rubin, G (2012) Thinking Sex: Notes for a Radical Theory of the Politics of Sexuality. In *Deviations* (pp 137–81). Durham, NC: Duke University Press.

Said, E (1978) *Orientalism*. New York: Pantheon Books.

Salovey, P and Mayer, J D (1990) Emotional Intelligence. *Imagination, Cognition and Personality*, 9(3): 185–211. https://doi.org/10.2190/DUGG-P24E-52WK-6CDG.

Saul, J R (2015) *The Comeback: How Aboriginals Are Reclaiming Power and Influence*. Toronto: Penguin.

Schein, E H (1992) *Organizational Culture and Leadership*, 2nd ed. San Francisco, CA: Jossey-Bass.

Schön, D (1983) *The Reflective Practitioner: How Professionals Think in Action*. London: Temple Smith.

Schwartz, B, Ben-Haim, Y and Dacso, C (2010) What Makes a Good Decision? Robust Satisficing as a Normative Standard of Rational Decision Making. *Journal for the Theory of Social Behaviour*, 41(2): 211–27.

Schwitzgebel, E (2024) Introspection. In Zalta, E N and Nodelman, U (eds) *The Stanford Encyclopedia of Philosophy*. Stanford, CA: Stanford University Press.

Sedgwick, E K (1990) *Epistemology of the Closet*. Berkeley, CA: University of California Press.

Šen, H, Begičević, N and Gerić, S (2011) Decision Making on Customer Relationship Management Solution Using the Analytic Network Process. In *Proceedings of the ITI 2011, 33rd International Conference on Information Technology Interfaces* (pp 439–44).

Sentencing Council (2022) *Sentencing Guidelines: Overview of Recent Reforms*. London: Sentencing Council.

Shakur, T (2006) *The Rose that Grew from Concrete*. New York: Simon & Schuster.

Sherlock, R (1953) The Nonjudgmental Attitude in Social Casework. Master of Social Work (MSW) thesis, Loyola University Chicago. [online] Available at: https://ecommons.luc.edu/luc_theses/1268 (accessed 14 January 2024).

Shi, H, Chong, D, Yan, G and He, W (2015) A Semantic Query-based Approach for Management Decision-making. *Journal of Management Analytics*, 2(1): 53–71.

Sicora, A, Taylor, B J, Alfandari, R, Enosh, G et al (2021) Using Intuition in Social Work Decision Making. *European Journal of Social Work*, 24(5): 772–87.

Simon, H A (1956) Rational Choice and the Structure of the Environment. *Psychological Review*, 63(2): 129–38.

Simon, H A (1957) *Models of Man: Social and Rational*. Chichester: John Wiley & Sons.

Simon, H A (1987) Making Management Decisions: The Role of Intuition and Emotion. *Academy of Management Perspectives*, 1(1): 57–64.

Simon, H A (1992) What Is an Explanation of Behaviour? *Psychological Science*, 3(3): 150–61.

Smith, H (2018) *Introduction to World Religions*, 3rd ed. Minneapolis, MN: Fortress Press.

Social Care Institute for Excellence (SCIE) (2020) *Risk Identification and Virtual Interventions for Social Workers*. London: SCIE.

Social Work England (2021) Professional Standards. [online] Available at: www.socialworkengland.org.uk/standards/professional-standards (accessed 17 August 2023).

Spade, D (2015) *Normal Life*. Durham, NC: Duke University Press.

Stanovich, K E and West, R F (2000) Individual Differences in Reasoning: Implications for the Rationality Debate? *Behavioural and Brain Sciences*, 23(5): 645–65.

Stasser, G and Titus, W (1985) Pooling of Unshared Information in Group Decision Making: Biased Information Sampling during Discussion. *Journal of Personality and Social Psychology*, 48(6): 1467–78. https://doi.org/10.1037/0022-3514.48.6.1467.

Straussner, S L A, Senreich, E and Steen, J T (2018) Wounded Healers: A Multistate Study of Licensed Social Workers' Behavioral Health Problems. *Social Work*, 63(2): 125–33. https://doi.org/10.1093/sw/swy012.

Stryker, S and Whittle, S (2006) *The Transgender Studies Reader*. London: Routledge.

Thaler, R H (1999) Mental Accounting Matters. *Journal of Behavioural Decision Making*, 12(3): 183–206.

Thompson, N (2017) *Social Problems and Social Justice*. New York: Macmillan.

Theoi Project (nd) *Greek Mythology: Exploring Mythology in Classical Literature and Art*. [online] Available at: www.theoi.com (accessed 13 January 2024).

Triandis, H C (1995) *Individualism & Collectivism*. Boulder, CO: Westview Press.

Turban, E, Sharda, R, Delen, D and King, D (2011) *Business Intelligence: A Managerial Approach*, 2nd ed. Boston, MA: Pearson.

Tversky, A and Kahneman, D (1974) Judgment under Uncertainty: Heuristics and Biases. *Science*, 185(4157): 1124–31.

United Nations (1948) *Universal Declaration of Human Rights*. Geneva: United Nations.

Vroom, V H (2003) Educating Managers for Decision Making and Leadership. *Management Decision*, 41(10): 968–78. https://doi.org/10.1108/00251740310509490.

Weber, M (1968) *Economy and Society: An Outline of Interpretive Sociology*. Berkeley, CA: University of California Press.

Weber, M (2002 [1905]) *The Protestant Ethic and the Spirit of Capitalism*. Harmondsworth: Penguin.

Weekes, A P (2016) *Effective Personal and Professional Judgement in Anti-Oppressive Practice*. Bristol: Policy Press.

Weekes, A P (2020) The Complexities of Making Recommendations for Adoption and Fostering Panels: An Investigation of the Biographic and Professional Influences on Panel Members' Decision-making and Attitudes. Professional Doctorate thesis, Tavistock and Portman NHS Foundation Trust/University of East London. [online] Available at: https://repository.tavistockandportman.ac.uk/2481/1/Weekes%20-%20Complexities.pdf (accessed 2 August 2023).

Weekes, A P (2021) There's No Such Thing as Non-judgemental. *Professional Social Work*, May: 28–29. [online] Available at: https://openresearch.lsbu.ac.uk/item/8zqv7 (accessed 2 February 2025).

Weekes, A P (2022) The Biographic and Professional Influences on Adoption and Fostering Panel Members' Recommendation-making. *Adoption and Fostering*, 45(4): 382–97.

Weekes, A P (2023) Being Intentional about Intersectionality and Positionality. *Social Work Education*, 1–10. https://doi.org/10.1080/02615479.2023.2273259.

REFERENCES

Weekes, A P (2023) Increased Personal Awareness Increases Personal Effectiveness. *Effective Personal and Professional Judgement*. [online] Available at: https://eppj.org/ (accessed 2 April 2025).

Wengraf, T (2004) *The Biographic-Narrative Interpretive Method (BNIM): Shortguide*. [online] Available at: https://eprints.ncrm.ac.uk/id/eprint/30/1/Biographic-NarrativeInterpretiveMethodShortGuide.doc (accessed 3 February 2025).

West, C and Zimmerman, D H (1987) Doing Gender. *Gender & Society*, 1(2): 125–51.

Winnicott, D W (1953) Transitional Objects and Transitional Phenomena: A Study of the First Not Me Possession. *International Journal of Psychoanalysis*, 34(2): 89–97.

Winnicott, D W (1971) The Use of an Object and Relating through Identifications. In *Playing and Reality* (pp 86–94). London: Tavistock.

Wittgenstein, L (1953) *Philosophical Investigations*. Oxford: Blackwell.

X, M (1970) *By Any Means Necessary: Speeches, Interviews, and a Letter*. Pathfinder Books Ltd.

Young Minds (2018) *Understanding Trauma and Adversity*. [online] Available at: www.youngminds.org.uk/professional/resources/understanding-trauma-and-adversity (accessed 2 September 2024).

Youth Justice Board (2021) *Youth Justice Statistics: England and Wales, 2019–2020*. London: Youth Justice Board.

Index

Page numbers in *italics* and **bold** denote figures and tables, respectively.

4 × 4 × 4 model, *73*

Abelson, R P, 101
Aboriginal Australian culture, 30, 50
active listening, 75, 111–12
activity theory, 34
adultification, 108–9, 156
Adventists of the Seventh Day, **58**
adverse childhood experiences (ACEs), 125
Africa
    faiths and religions in, 48–9
    philosophies and key philosophers in, 14, 16–18, 112–13
ageism, 33–4
agnostics, 50, **59**
Alfred, Taiaiake, **22**
alternative worldviews, 14
amygdala, 87
anchoring bias, 115
ancient philosophy, 26
Anda, R, 125
Andean indigenous cultures, 24
anxiety, 115
Arendt, Hannah, **29**
Aristotle, **26**, 114
artificial intelligence, 89
Asia
    faiths and religions in, 48
    philosophies in, 14–15
atheism and atheists, 50, **57**
attachment theory, 44
attentive, critical, exploratory and iterative (ACEI) interactions, 123
Australasian philosophies, **30**, 30
averaging, as social decision scheme, 98
Aymara people, 24

Bailey, M, 107–8
Banks, S, 154
Baron, J, 7
basic assumption group, 6–7
Beauvoir, Simone de, **29**
Becker, H, 36
beliefs, 79. *See also* faiths and religions
    impact on thinking, 8
    and sociology, 39–40
Bentham, Jeremy, 114
biases, 7, 32, 84, 130, 150, 151
    cognitive biases, 115
    confirmation bias, 84, 102, 115
    examples, 75
    implicit, 8
    pre-decisional distortion in evidence processing, 7
Biestek, F P, 11
Biographic Narrative Interpretive Method (BNIM), 6
biographies, impact on decision-making, 9, 31
Bion, W, 6–7, 32–3, 103
Black women, 107–8
Bodenhausen, G V, 7
Bolen, J, 72
bolstering tactic, 100
Bornstein, B H, 7
Borton's framework, 129
bounded rationality, 86
British Association of Social Workers (BASW)
    Code of Ethics, 149, 151, 152
    PCF. *See* Professional Capabilities Framework (PCF)
Brookfield's reflective model, 131–2
Buddhism, 15, 48, 50, **52**
Buen Vivir, 24
Burke, B, 151
business, EPPJ application in, 158–9

capitalist class, 34
Carlson, K A, 7
Carmichael, Stokely, 109
Catholicism, 49, 50, **53**
Charcot, J-M, 125
child protection conference, 105
Children Act (2004), 104, 106
Christianity, 48, 49, 50
Church of Jesus Christ of Latter-Day Saints, **61**
cisnormativity, 41
civil partnership status, 37
classism, 34–5
codependency, 70
coexisting with nature, 24
cognition, and EPPJ, 115
cognitive abilities, 83
cognitive biases, 115
cognitive competencies, 89
cognitive psychology, 95, 114
    analytical (cognitive) skills, 8
    cognitive-behavioural approaches, 44
collaborative approach, 72
collective decision-making, 6–7

INDEX

collectivism, 24, 85
Collins, P H, 40
communalism, 14, 16
community, sense of, 144
compassion fatigue, 71
complex experiences, 125–6
computer-based decision support systems, 99–100
confirmation bias, 84, 102, 115
conflict theory, 34–5, 38
Confucianism, **15**
conscious, concept of, 31
consciousness/constructiveness axle, 67–9, 141–3
  categories, 75
  complexities, 125–6
  and EPPJ development, 124–5
  examples, 75–6
consensus decision-making, 97
consequentialism, 114
consult method, 99
container–contained concept, 103
context, and EPPJ, 116
corporate social responsibility (CSR), 88, 159
countertransference, 68, 70, 73
Crenshaw, K, 108
criminal justice settings
  EPPJ application in, 156–8
  policy and practice, EPPJ impact on, 158
crisis trigger, 70
critical race theory (CRT), 38–9
critical reflection, 74, 113, 117, 131, 156
critical theory, 107
critical thinking, 44, 89, 111, 115–16, 154, 158
cultural dimensions theory, 85
cultural humility, 30, 64, 72, 151, 160
culture, influence on decision-making, 85
Cumming, E, 34

Dalrymple, J, 151
Daoism, **15**, 15, 50, **51**
Davies, A J H, 108–9
Davis, Angela, **20**
de la Fuente-Núñez, V, 34
decide method, 99
decision support systems, 89
decision-making. *See also* group decision making
  anatomy of, 93–4
  collaborative decision-making, 144
  complexity of, 1
  consensus, 97
  ethical decision-making, 112, 118, 132, 134, 150

  group decision support systems (GDSS), 99–101
  individual and collective, 6–7
  intuitive decision-making, 102
  judge and jury, comparison between, 7
  majority decision-making, 97
  moral decision-making, 134
  normative model, 99
  organisational, 87–8
  rational decision-making, 101–2
  skills, enhancement of, 88–9
  social decision schemes, 98–9
  theories related to, 7
  voting-based method, 97
decision-making, affecting factors
  amygdala, 87
  biases and heuristics, 84
  bounded rationality, 86
  cognitive abilities, 83–4
  corporate social responsibility, 88
  cultural values and practices, 85
  culture of organisations, 87
  dual-process theories, 86
  economic conditions, 85
  emotional states, 83–4
  environmental factors, 85
  ethical leadership, 88
  ethics, 88
  group dynamics, 84
  hierarchical structures in organisations, 87
  individual factors, 83–4
  moral frameworks, 88
  neurobiological perspectives, 86–7
  personality traits, 84
  prefrontal cortex (PFC), 86–7
  psychological theories and models, 86
  rational choice theory, 86
  situational context, 85
  social factors, 84–5
  social norms, 84
  stakeholder interests, 88
  striatum, 87
  technological advancements, 85
delegation, as social decision scheme, 98, 99
deontological ethics, 88, 114
deontology, 114
Derrida, Jacques, **29**
Descartes, René, **27**
Dewey, John, **19**, 112
dialectic method, 111
disabilities (physical/mental), 35–6
discrimination, 126, 151, 152, 154
  anti-discrimination laws, 108, 153
  intersectionality, 108

non-discrimination, 154
  racial, 39, 107
disengagement theory, 34
diversity, and EPPJ, 151
Dominelli, L, 151
Dreamtime concept, 30
Driscoll, J, 129
dual-process theories, 86, 114
Durkheim, Émile, 34, 35, 39–40

economic conditions, impact on decision-making, 85
education, and EPPJ, 118
effective judgement
  in business, 158
  in criminal justice settings, 156–7
  in diversity and difference, 151
  in finance, 159
  in healthcare, 156
  in legislative frameworks, 154
  in Professional Capabilities Framework (PCF), 152–3
  in values and ethics, 150
Effective Personal Professional Judgement. *See* EPPJ (Effective Personal Professional Judgement)
emotional competencies, 89
emotional intelligence, 74, 89, 115, 125, 139
emotional (intuitive) thinking, 8
Emotional Quotient (EQ), 125
emotions, 31, 87, 89, 130, 132, 148
  and EPPJ, 115
  impact on decision-making, 83–4
  management of, 103
empathy, 71, 89, 139
empowerment, 72, 111
engagement, 72
enrichment, 72
environmental factors, and decision-making, 89
EPPJ (Effective Personal Professional Judgement)
  and active listening, 111
  and adultification, 108–9
  and Korthagen and Vasalos onion model, comparison between, 134–5
  and Borton's framework, comparison between, 129
  and Brookfield's reflective model, comparison, 131–2
  and cognition, 115
  consciousness/constructiveness axle, 141–3
  contextual factors, 116
  development of, 6–9
  and dialectic method, 111
  emergence of, 5
  and emotions, 115
  and empowerment, 111
  and ethics, 111, 114, 116, 131, 149–50
  and Fook's inductive process, comparison between, 133–4
  and Gibbs's Reflective Cycle, 132–3
  and institutional racism, 109
  and internalised oppression, 116–17
  and intersectionality, 108
  and judgement, 114
  and Kolb's learning model, comparison between, 129–30
  and language theory, 110
  and liberation, 111
  and liberation and decolonisation, 112
  MacLean's daisy values model, comparison between, 135–6
  and misogynoir, 107–8
  and moral courage, 116
  and power dynamics, 113
  and pragmatism, 112
  and psychosocial development theory, 113
  purpose of, 41
  and reflective practices, 112
  and reflective process, comparison between, 131
  and structural racism, 109–10
  sub-categories of, 144–5
  Systems 1 and 2 thinking, 114
  and Ubuntu, 113
  and values, 149–50
EPPJ application, 107, 149
  blue dimension, 145
  in business, 158–9
  diversity and difference, 151–2
  in finance, 159–60
  first step in, 143–5
  green zone, 146
  in healthcare, 156
  higher education (HE) and teaching, 154–5
  legislative frameworks, 153–4
  in police/courts and criminal justice settings, 156–8
  and Professional Capabilities Framework (PCF), 152–3
  red sphere, 146
  testimonies, 145–6
  to values and ethics, 150
  yellow corner, 145
EPPJ assertions
  complexities, 125–6
  prejudging, 126–7
  reflective practitioner, becoming a, 128
  self-awareness, 124–5

EPPJ category, 141, 147–8
  first step in identification of, 143–5
  in practice, 145–6
  questionnaire, **144**
  research involved, 141–3
EPPJ development
  consciousness/constructiveness axle, 124–5
  education and training strategies, 118
  effectiveness in work situations, improvement of, 136–7
  mentorship and role models, 118–19
  personal performance improvement, 136
  and reflective practice, 119–20
Equality Act (2010), 33, 153, 154
equitability, 72
Erikson, Erik, 113
ethical challenges (case study), 42, 43
ethical decision-making, 44, 88, 114, 134, 149–50, 158
  corporate social responsibility, 88
  and EPPJ, 116, 131
  ethical leadership, 88
  moral frameworks, 88
ethical judgement, 116
ethical leadership, 111–12
Europe
  faiths and religions in, 50
  philosophies and key philosophers in, 25–9
European Convention on Human Rights, 41
experiential learning, 118, 120, 130, 133

facilitate method, 99
F.A.I.T.H. Assessment Tool, 63
faiths and religions, 47–8. *See also* beliefs
  in Africa, 48–9
  in Asia, 48
  case study, 65
  in Europe, 50
  in North America, 49
  in Oceania, 50
  and sociology, 39–40
  in South America, 49–50
family history, 144
family network meetings, 105
Fanon, Frantz, **23**, 112
Felitti, V, 125
feminism, 40, 108
finance, EPPJ application in, 159–60
Finlay, L, 34
Five-Factor Model, 84
Foley, L A, 7
Fook's inductive process, 133–4

foster and adoption panels, 105
Freire, Paulo, **25**, 111
Freud, Sigmund, 31, 32
Freudian slips, 31
Functionalism, 37

Galen, 35
Garnham, Neil, 104
gathering approach, 97
Gautama Buddha, **15**
gender inequality, 40–1
gender reassignment, 36
Gibbs's reflective cycle, 132–3
Gilbert, P, 69
Gilligan, Carol, **20**
Goleman, D, 125
Greene, E, 7
group belonging, sense of, 144
group decision support systems (GDSS), 97–8, 99–101
group decision-making
  definition of, 95
  group consensus process, 96–9
  versus individual decision making, 101
  information-sharing issues in, 101
  managing emotions within, 103
  psychological research on groups, 95–6
  social identity approach, 96
  within social work practice, 102–3
group dynamics, 6, 84
group performance, 95
group-level behavioural phenomenon, 6–7
groups
  basic assumption group, 6–7
  definition of, 94–5
  influence on thinking, 8
  tactics for avoiding making decision, 100
  workgroup, 6
groupthink, 1, 7, 8, 9, 84, 96–7

Hackney model, 103
Hall, Stuart, **23**
Hamilton, Charles V, 109
Harris, Leonard, **21**
Hastie, R, 7
Hau'ofa, Epeli, **31**
healthcare, EPPJ application in, 156
Hegel, Georg Wilhelm Friedrich, **28**
Henry, W E, 34
heuristics, 83, 84, 85, 114, 115
hierarchical structures, in organisation, 87
higher education (HE) and teaching, EPPJ in, 154–5

INDEX

high-stakes environments, influence on decision-making, 85
Hinduism, 15, 48, 50, **51**
Hippocrates, **27**, 35, 125
holding concept, 103
Holy Book, 47
hooks, bell, **21**
Howard, Elbert, **20**
Human Rights Act (1998), 153
Hume, David, **28**
Hypatia, **16**

identity formation, 29
implicit biases, 8
individual decision-making, 6–7
    and awareness of values and beliefs, 8
    versus group decision-making, 101
individualism, 85
institutional racism, 109
intelligent decision support systems (IDSS), 99, 100
internalised oppression, 116–17
interpretive sociology, 34, 35
intersectionality, 108
introspection, 123, 129, 130–2, 134–5, 138
intuition, 8, 101, 102
irrational thinking, 7
Islam, 48, 49, 50, **54**

Jainism, 52
Janis, I L, 7, 96–7
Jehovah Witnesses, **58**
Judaism, 49, 50, **52**
judgement, concept of, 114
judges
    comparison between, 7
    decision-making process, 1
Jung, Carl G, 9, 66–7, 125
jurors, decision-making process, 1
jury, comparison between, 7

Kant, Immanuel, **28**, 114
Kheiron myth, 65–6, 67
Klein, M, 32
Kocc (Kotch) Barma Fall, **16**
Kolb's experiential learning model, 129–30
Korthagen and Vasalos onion model, 134–5

labelling theory, 36
language. *See also* symbolic interactionism
language, and social work practice, 110
Laozi (Lao Tzu), 15
Latin American philosophies, 14
leadership styles, 116
Levi, A, 101

liberation
    and decolonisation, 112
    pedagogy of, 111
'link' in thinking, 6
Locke, John, **27**
Lord, L, 7

Mackay, T, 69
MacLean's daisy values model, 135–6
Macpherson Report (1999), 109
majority decision-making, 97
managerial decision-making, 101, 102
Mangena, Mugabe R M K Z (Rashid) N K, **18**
Māori community, 30
marriage status, 37
Martí, José, **24**
Marx, Karl, 34, 39
maternity, sociological theories, 37–8
Mayer, J D, 125
Mbembe, Achille, **18**
McAdams, D P, 125
medical model of disability, 35
mentorship, and EPPJ, 118–19, 120
microaggressions, 126
Middleton, R, 34
Mill, John Stuart, **28**, 114
Miller, P, 7, 109–10
misogynoir, 107–8
modern philosophy, 27
modus operandi (MO), 128
moral courage, 116
moral frameworks, impact on decision-making, 88
Mormonism, **58**
Morrisons, T, 73

narrative identity, 125
Newcomb, M, 69
Newton, Huey P, **20**
Nietzsche, Friedrich, **29**, 113
Nkrumah, Kwame, **17**
non-judgemental attitude, 11, 124, 126
North America
    faiths and religions in, 49
    philosophies and key philosophers in, 19
North American philosophies, **19–23**

Oceania
    faiths and religions in, 50
    philosophies and key philosophers in, 30
Oceanian philosophies, **30**
Offender Assessment System (OASys), 158
Oliver, M, 36
Olúwọlé, Sophie Bosede, **18**

open communication, 116
organisational culture, 116, 147
organisational decision-making, 87–8
  hierarchical structure, 87
  organisational culture, 87
  stakeholder interests, 88
organisational psychology, 95
Orthodox communities, 50
Oruka, H O, 112–13
over-confidence bias, 84, 115
Oxhandler, H K, 39

panel recommendation-making, 9
panel recommendation-making process, 8, 11
Parkinson's law, 100
Parsons, Talcott, 34, 35
pedagogical approaches, 111
Pennington, N, 7
Pentecostalism, **59**
personal biography
  complexities, 125
  impact of, 124–5
  at work, examples, 75–6
personal judgement, 117
  in business, 159
  in criminal justice settings, 157
  in diversity and difference, 151–2
  in finance, 159
  in healthcare, 156
  in legislative frameworks, 154
  in Professional Capabilities Framework (PCF), 153
  in values and ethics, 150
personality traits, impact on decision-making, 84
philosophic sagacity, 112–13
philosophy, 13, 14, 44
  ancient philosophy, 26
  in different countries, 14–30
  modern philosophy, 27
  postmodern philosophy, 29, 37
  related to social work practice, 110–14
phronesis, 114
Pigott, M A, 7
pilgrimage, 47
Plato, **26**
Platt, L, 34
plurality, as social decision scheme, 98
police/courts, EPPJ application in, 156–8
postcolonialism, 38
postmodern philosophy, 29
postmodern theory, 37
post-traumatic stress disorder (PTSD), 125
power dynamics, 29, 69, 113, 151
pragmatism, 112

preference-aggregation paradigm, 95
prefrontal cortex (PFC), 86–7
pregnancy, sociological theories, 37–8
prejudging, 126–7
probation and parole settings, 158
procrastination tactic, 100
professional background, 144
professional boundaries maintenance, 71
Professional Capabilities Framework (PCF), 149, 152, 160
professional judgement, 95, 118
  in business, 159
  in criminal justice settings, 157–8
  in diversity and difference, 152
  in finance, 159–60
  in healthcare, 156
  in legislative frameworks, 154
  in Professional Capabilities Framework (PCF), 153
  in values and ethics, 150
professional presentation, 144
professionalism, 6, 8, 126, 152, 160
projection identification, 31
projective identification, 32
Protestantism, **55**
psychology, 14, 44, 94
  analytical, 67
  bounded rationality, 86
  and cognition. *See* cognitive psychology
  concepts in, 31–3
  dual-process theories, 86
  organisational psychology, 95
  rational choice theory, 86
  social identity approach, 96
  social psychology, 95
  sub-disciplines research study on groups, 95–6
psychosocial development theory, 113
Ptahhotep, **16**, 111–12

Quaker (aka Religious Society of Friends), **56**
Quechua people, 24
Queer theory, 36, 41

racism, 38–9, 107
  institutional racism, 76, 109
  structural racism, 109–10
  systemic racism, 39
Ramose, M B, 113
Randall, Uncle Bob, **30**
range voting methods, 97
Rastafarianism, 49, 50, **60**
rational choice theory, 86
rational decision making, 101–2
rationality, 101

Rawls, John, **19**
Reason, J, 99
reclaiming social work, 103
recommendation-making
 process, 68, 79
reflection-for-action, 123
reflection-in-action, 123
reflection-on-action, 123
reflective practice, 112, 117, 119, 120, 123,
 128, 130, 138, 150, 151, 155, 157, 158
 Brookfield's reflective model
 (1988), 131-2
 case study, 119-20
 and EPPJ, 119-20
 Fook's inductive process, 133-4
 Gibbs's reflective cycle, 132-3
 reflective process, 129, 131
reflective process, *131*, 136
reflexivity, 151, 160
religions. *See* faiths and religions
Resnik, M D, 102
responsibility denial, in group
 decision-making, 100
Robert, Cyril Lionel, **22**
role models, and EPPJ, 118-19
Rolfe, G, 129
Russo, J E, 7

Salovey, P, 125
Sánchez, Luis Alberto, **24**
Sarra, Chris, **31**
Saul, John Ralston, **21**
Schön, D, 129
Scientology, 50, **61**
Seale, Bobby, **20**
self, sense of, 32, 36, 125, 144
self-awareness, 75, 89, 123, 129, 131, 132,
 134, 135, 138, 144, 150, 154, 155, 157
 emotional, 68
 and EPPJ, 117, 124-5
 and reflective process, 119
sexual orientation, sociological
 theories, 41
sexuality, 40-1
Sherlock, R, 79
Sikhism, 48, **55**
Simon, H A, 86
Simpson, Leanne Betasamosake, **22**
Singer, Peter, **31**
situational context, impact on decision-
 making, 85
social decision schemes, 98-9
social identity approach, 96
social institutions, impact of, 151
social justice scholarship, 107

social loafing, 95
social norms, impact on decision-making, 84
social secularism, 50
sociology, 14, 33, 44
 and age, 33-4
 and belief systems, 39-40
 and class, 34-5
 and disabilities (physical/mental), 35-6
 and gender reassignment, 36
 and gender and sex, 40-1
 and marriage and civil partnership
 status, 37
 and maternity and pregnancy, 37-8
 and race, 38-9
 and sexual orientation, 41
 societal causality, 33
Socrates, **26**, 111
somatic marker hypothesis, 84
South African philosophies, 113
South America
 faiths and religions in, 49-50
 philosophies and key philosophers
 in, 23-7
spiritism, 49, **57**
splitting process, 32
stakeholder interests, impact on
 decision-making, 88
Stickley, T, 69
Straussner, S L A, 69
stress, 115
striatum, 87
structural functionalism, 34, 35
structural racism, 109-10
sub-committees, 98
supervision, significance of, 151
symbolic interactionism, 37-8, 40
System 1 thinking, 114
System 2 thinking, 114
systemic oppression, 38
systemic unit models, 103

Taoism, **15**, 50, **51**
technology
 impact on decision-making, 85
 use of, 89
thinking, 31, 68, 79
 Bion's concept of, 32-3
 conscious and unconscious, 1, 6
 critical, 44
 intuitive (emotional) thinking, 8
 irrational, 7
 'link' in, 6
Thompson, N, 152
Thompson's PCS model, 151
'thoughts without a thinker', 32

time pressure, influence on decision-making, 85
training programmes, and EPPJ, 118
transgenders, 41
triviality, law of, 100
Two-Spirit Identity concept, 30

Ubuntu, 16, 113
unanimity, as social decision scheme, 98
unconscious, concept of, 31
Unitarian Universalism, 50, **62**
Universal Declaration of Human Rights, UN, 41
utilitarianism, 88, 114

values, 79, 149–50
  awareness, impact on thinking, 8
  -based dialogue and judgements, 127
Vodou, 49
voting-based methods, of decision-making, 97, 98

Weber, Max, 34, 35, 39
Weekes, A P, 5, 31–2, 75, 128, 141, 145, 147, 149, 154
Wengraf, T, 6
West, Cornel, **22**
Western philosophies, 14
Winnicott, D W, 103
Wiredu, Kwasi, **17**

Wittgenstein, L, 110
womanism, 40, 41
Wonnacott, J, 73
workgroup, 6
working class, 34, 39
wounded healer, *68*, 79–80, 125
  addressing issues of, 72
  case study, 75–6
  concept of, 65
  consciousness/constructiveness axle, 67–9
  Greek mythology root, 65–6
  and Jung, 66–7
  and modern thinkers, 67
  negative impact of, 70–1
  positive impact of, 71–2
  recognising, 75–6
  recognition of, 74
  in social work training and practice, 69
  supervisors support, 73
  supporting, 74–5
  university lecturers support, 74
Wyer Jr, R, 7

Yacob, Zera, **17**
Yerkes–Dodson law, 115
Young Minds (2018), 125

Zea, Leopoldo, **25**
Zoroastrianism, **51**